"Apostle Kathryn Krick has writtei believers about anointing. Spiritual snipers w... dangerous against the enemy of our souls for the Kingdom of Jesus Christ to destroy the works of darkness. This amazing book will truly bless brothers and sisters around the world."

Evangelist John Ramirez, John Ramirez Ministries

"When you read *The Secret of the Anointing*, you'll be infused with revelation on what the power of the anointing is, the way in which it is received and how God desires to use us as Kingdom movers, shakers and breakers in the Spirit. Prepare to dispel darkness and glorify Jesus Christ. You won't regret reading this book!"

Apostle Charlie Shamp, Destiny Encounters International, author of *Angels*, *Transfigured*, *Altars* and *Mystical Prayer*

"*The Secret of the Anointing* is a game changer. This book will open your eyes to exactly what God has placed inside each one of us to flow in another realm of anointing! Everybody needs this book in their library."

Kim Jones "Real Talk Kim," pastor of Limitless Church, Atlanta

"I absolutely love Kathryn Krick. This book is so necessary right now; people are hungry for revival and to see a move of God. Her testimony speaks to the power of God. I love the honesty, humility and authority she carries. This book is a tool for believers to understand what God has done and what He desires to do through us. I can't wait for the world to be blessed by this literary work."

Erica Campbell, Grammy-nominated singer and songwriter

"Kathryn Kuhlman once said that anyone who was willing to pay the price could have the same anointing she had. Decades later, we see how God has raised up another Kathryn sharing a similar message. Kathryn is a pure-hearted lover of Jesus, and many have encountered freedom and deliverance through her ministry. She has overcome setbacks, challenges and criticisms, and has been vigilant to keep her eyes upon Jesus. I pray that as you read *The Secret of the Anointing* you will receive fresh impartation to live as a consecrated lover of Jesus."

Jennifer Miskov, Ph.D., founding director of School
of Revival, author of *Fasting for Fire*, *Ignite Azusa*,
*Walking on Water* and others

"*The Secret of the Anointing* is timely. It is troubling to see many in the church and in leadership reject the anointing of the Holy Spirit when in the Bible the criteria for ministry includes anointing. To be anointed means to be supernaturally empowered to do the impossible! Nothing in ministry is possible without the anointing. Apostle Kathryn brings a restoration of this important revelation of the anointing to the Church. She defines what the anointing is, the cost of the anointing and how to release and maintain it. This powerful book will transform and change your life so you can start moving in the supernatural power of God with miracles, signs and wonders. I highly recommend this book!"

Apostle Guillermo Maldonado, King Jesus
International Ministry

# THE
# SECRET
## OF THE
# ANOINTING

# THE
# SECRET
## OF THE
# ANOINTING

### ACCESSING THE POWER OF GOD
### TO WALK IN MIRACLES

## KATHRYN KRICK

**Chosen**

a division of Baker Publishing Group
Minneapolis, Minnesota

Published by Chosen Books
Minneapolis, Minnesota
www.chosenbooks.com

Chosen Books is a division of
Baker Publishing Group, Grand Rapids, Michigan

Printed in the United States of America

Library of Congress Cataloging-in-Publication Data
Names: Krick, Kathryn, 1991– author.
Title: The secret of the anointing : accessing the power of God to walk in miracles / Kathryn Krick.
Description: Minneapolis, Minnesota : Chosen Books, a division of Baker Publishing Group, [2023]
Identifiers: LCCN 2022059796 | ISBN 9780800763299 (trade paper) | ISBN 9780800763381 (casebound) | ISBN 9781493442034 (ebook)
Subjects: LCSH: Anointing of the Holy Spirit. | Demoniac possession. | Healing—Religious aspects.
Classification: LCC BT123 .K75 2023 | DDC 234/.13—dc23/eng/20230308
LC record available at https://lccn.loc.gov/2022059796

Cover design by LOOK Design Studio

Baker Publishing Group publications use paper produced from sustainable forestry practices and post-consumer waste whenever possible.

23   24   25   26   27   28   29        8   7   6   5   4   3   2

# CONTENTS

# FOREWORD

I have studied revival figures throughout history for much of my ministry life. What does it take to carry the power and presence of God's anointing? Why did certain people emerge in the time they did to bring Christianity forward? How does one become qualified for this? These questions have driven me on a quest for a lot of my Christian life.

This curiosity and pursuit has also led me to believe that, in my lifetime, multitudes of Christians are being appointed and are going to rise up to deal with some of the most pressing issues of our generation, but with the anointing of God. The options we have on the table of humanity to deal with social justice, racial issues, climate and environmental issues, politics and even some of the issues that are plaguing the church are not enough. We need God options—options that only those who walk in intimacy with and empowerment from God can bring. I am believing that God is igniting believers all over the world to walk in His fresh anointing to not only deal with the massive oppressions of the demonic but also to usher in the Kingdom activity that Jesus' great price on the cross is worthy of.

The beautiful thing about God's secrets when it comes to moving in authority, and especially when it comes to moving in His power and anointing, is that they are all gained through Christ, and this gained knowledge is transferable. Each person who advances in their faith can ignite or impart to others. God made believers to be catalytic for one another. He made our faith to see breakthrough, deliverance and visitation, and revival comes by hearing (see Romans 10:17).

In light of this truth, I went to see Kathryn in the park where she was holding services because I had heard some amazing reports (and even some controversial ones) and was just hungry to see what God was doing. Los Angeles was in total lockdown, and my wife and I were trying to navigate the politics of mask wearing in our city and public exposure for our family to a sickness that we didn't have a lot of information about, so I was excited to hear about a ministry that was wide open in the park while most of our friends in the city had shut down their churches and meetings. Los Angeles is one of the most cautious places on the Earth when it comes to political and social norms, and I didn't know of any other church that was promising to pursue the presence of God in live meetings in Hollywood or central LA at that time; I knew this was profound.

The service hadn't started yet, and Kathryn was helping her team and being refreshingly approachable to everyone who was coming from what seemed to be some pretty far-off places. When she started preaching, the level of down-to-earth connection to her message and to the people who attended felt very special. As I watched people manifest demons and Kathryn effortlessly help them into freedom through the anointing, I knew I was witnessing something that I have been praying for more of: God had raised Kathryn up, and she was helping to raise others up. I say it was something special because I could hear in Kathryn's own messages—whether online or in her meetings—that her drive is to raise up the average Christian who really wants to walk with God into the same kinds of gifts, anointing and authority. She wasn't trying to be the only one, and there was no ego in the meeting. She was simply gracefully moving in her calling and office, imparting freedom to others or declaring and praying that they could move in the anointing and walk in revival now.

I was so excited because, with all the years that I have gone out of personal hunger to investigate the miraculous and those who walk in prophetic and powerful callings, I knew this was legitimate. Kathryn has the marks of a true apostolic person, which is to activate others in the anointing. When she teaches, she makes it all seem so simple, like any of us can walk in the anointing of Christ, which is so true but not always realized!

As I write this foreword, I have to say that this book is so inclusive and practical. It dug deep into that core place in my spirit that just wants more of Jesus and to walk in His manifest reality while here on Earth. If you picked up this book, it's because you are hungry (or want to be) for the same, and Kathryn has laid out a very practical guide that is easy to follow and biblically based.

If you pursue God to walk in His anointing, there will always be some stigma, whether that is controversy with other Christian groups, judgement from other leaders, gossip and slander from people at work or in your career or family misunderstanding. There is a price, and that price sometimes gets amplified the more God's anointing increases on you. But I want to encourage you that no other relationship or earthly function can bring such a fulfillment as walking with the Spirit of God in His power to bring His original plans and design to His people. There isn't a drug that can make you feel so high, there isn't an earthly relational connection that can make you feel so loved. This is a unique experience that God designed all of us for, but few will actually attain it because the price is so high. Kathryn is paying that price, and because of it, she is seeing the powerful presence of God do things that are rare and miraculous. This could be your story, too.

Read the full book, take notes, ask the Holy Spirit what He is requiring of you. Picture your life with the anointing, picture yourself moving in deliverance and miracle power, envision yourself leading people to freedom and declaring powerful words from God, and then ask God to make you the person it will take to carry that anointing. He wants to give you more than His love and His salvation; He wants to raise you up and use your life to bring Jesus His full reward!

Shawn Bolz
Host of *The Shawn Bolz Show*, *Exploring the*
*Marketplace*, *Exploring the Prophetic*
Author of *Wired to Hear*, *Translating God*, *Encounter*
www.bolzministries.com

# INTRODUCTION

## *Revival Broke Out*

I was on my way to "Revival in the Park" on a Sunday morning in mid-March 2021. My car was full of all our outdoor church equipment. I was about to set up for Sunday service with our team of two—Jeanntal, our worship leader (now my assistant and best friend), plus me. I was sitting in the car, talking to God, so full of expectancy that He would move in power like never before. There were four people who had informed me that they were traveling across the country, two from Nashville and two from Massachusetts, to come to Five-Fold Church (or 5F Church, as we call it) for our service in the park.

I had been the pastor/apostle of 5F Church for about four years at that point. Our congregation had gone from twenty people in 2017, to fifteen people in 2018, to ten people in 2019, to sometimes just two people in 2020 (Jeanntal and me in the park), when we took services outside because we could no longer rent our building due to Covid. I had been believing in a promise from God, a prophecy spoken to me more than four years prior, that He would do many miracles through me and that I was called to reach the nations as an apostle of Jesus Christ. At 5F Church we had also been believing in a prophecy released to us in 2017 that *Revival Is Now* for America, and that it would begin in Los Angeles and spread across the United States and the world.

But for three years I didn't see many miracles happen at our church (at least, I didn't see what I imagined revival to look like), and our church decreased in numbers each year. Yet I never stopped believing in the promises of God and declaring that *Revival Is Now*. I didn't have much of a following on social media up to this point, either (around a thousand Instagram followers, a few hundred YouTube subscribers and a few thousand TikTok followers).

On December 30, 2020, I created and posted a one-minute video on TikTok showing God moving in power the previous year at 5F Church. In 2020, I had seen Him heal Tanzanian children who had HIV, and heal others who had leg pain. I saw His power touch people so mightily that they fell back. I put these miracles in the video and prayed for the viewers at the end of it. A couple of days later, on January 1, 2021—my thirtieth birthday—the video reached one million views. I was completely shocked! Talk about a birthday surprise!

And then I read the comments. There were thousands of comments, each one testifying of miracles people had received while they watched the video. Healings, deliverances, people feeling the power of God, even atheists testifying that they felt power as they watched the video. I had only seen one person testify of receiving a miracle through any of my videos online before this, and that was two months prior. Now there were thousands testifying after just a one-minute video?

That video, and some additional videos I made, started circulating and going viral, and they reached these people in Massachusetts and Nashville. On that Sunday in mid-March 2021, these four flew in to come to "Revival in the Park." Although online there were thousands viewing my livestreams, our park revival services were still small. They had increased from five people the first week in January 2021 to about twenty-five to thirty by mid-March. I couldn't believe four people were flying across the country to come to our church service in the park, and there were fewer than thirty of us there!

I was on my way to church that day full of expectation because I knew this principle in the Kingdom of God: When people are hungry and sacrifice for God (for example, by traveling across the country), God shows up. He satisfies the thirsty and fills the hungry with good things (see Psalm 107:9). I had expectancy that this would be the most powerful service we had ever had, and that we would see God move extraordinarily. But I had no idea what God was actually about to do and how this one Sunday would change the course of my entire life. It would be the day that the walls of Jericho would come down and the promise I had been waiting on and meditating on just about daily for four and a half years would finally come to pass!

I showed up to the park's amphitheater and found sixty people from some sort of social event gathered in our spot. We couldn't reserve it at the time because of Covid; it was just first come, first served. Although their event was wrapping up, they didn't want to move. We had never had the amphitheater taken before. On this day of all days! It was a spiritual battle to have church. I pleaded with the group, and finally they moved to the side of the amphitheater. But they still continued to blast heavy metal music and socialize just six feet from where I was preaching.

I told those who had traveled cross-country to be there to come up to the front row and I would preach loudly over the heavy metal music. I became even more expectant because I knew the devil was trying harder than ever to stop these hungry children of God from receiving. After the message, I started praying for one of the girls from Massachusetts. She told me,

"What made me come was that when I watched one of your videos, I saw Jesus in your eyes."

I started praying for this woman, and without me touching her, she fell back with the power of God. I had seen God move in that way as I had ministered before, but then I started noticing something different. Instead of lying peacefully on the ground, her body was trembling and convulsing. I immediately discerned that this was a demon trembling in her. I had never seen this when I ministered before. I had seen other ministers cast out demons, but I had never seen demons tremble in my ministry!

The Holy Spirit led me to address the demon sternly, with authority, and command it to leave her. When I did, the demon spoke through her mouth: "I don't want her to preach" (meaning this woman the demon was speaking out of). I commanded the demon to then stand up. The girl stood up—or the demon possessing her body stood her up, forced to obey the command because Jesus has given us authority over demons. I then commanded it to leave her. As soon as I said the words, the demon left, and the force of the demon leaving her body made her fall down, as if someone had pushed her hard. Her head fell perfectly onto one congregant's foot, and she was immediately asleep. It was just like in Luke 4:35–36:

> "Be quiet!" Jesus said sternly. "Come out of him!" Then the demon threw the man down before them all and came out without injuring him.
>
> All the people were amazed and said to each other, "What words these are! With authority and power he gives orders to impure spirits and they come out!"

This was the first time I saw the anointing in me make demons tremble and be cast out. From there, it was as if the floodgates opened. Every single Sunday since that day, demons have trembled and been cast out of multitudes of people. The video of the first demon being cast out went viral, and within a couple of weeks, people were flying in from different states to encounter God and be set free at 5F Church's "Revival in the Park" services. From that Sunday in mid-March to Sunday, May 23, the church grew from twenty-five to seventy people. On May 30, three hundred people came! Since that Sunday, hundreds have come every week, and every single week people have flown in from different states and countries (for example, from Tahiti, Romania, Japan, the United Kingdom, Colombia, Australia, the Dominican Republic, Spain, Turkey, Mexico, Canada, the Netherlands, Malaysia, Singapore and India). Thousands have been delivered in person at 5F Church and also just by watching the services online.

By August 2021, I was traveling every single week to different states to minister at conferences and "Revival Is Now" events, and many people were delivered, healed and received many miracles at every service. In January 2022, I began traveling to different countries to minister (ten nations in 2022), and we saw God move everywhere in His same extraordinary power. Now, people in different time zones wake up in the middle of the night to tune in to our live events and encounter Jesus!

I started out not knowing that Jesus was still using people to cast out demons, heal the sick and do signs and wonders, and not imagining that God would ever use me to do those things. Then I went to believing that God would use me in His power, but never seeing it for years. Then one day, I started seeing the power of God move through me in ways that shocked me daily!

In this book, I am going to share the secrets I have learned about the anointing. It is God's will for all of His children to walk in His power. It is my assignment from God to share these secrets with you, so that you are able to access the anointing as well. *Revival Is Now*, and God is ready to use you in power, in ways that will shock you!

"And these signs will accompany those who believe: In my name they will drive out demons; they will speak in new tongues; they will pick up snakes with their hands; and when they drink deadly poison, it will not hurt them at all; they will place their hands on sick people, and they will get well."

Mark 16:17–18

# 1

# What Is the Anointing?

And it shall come to pass in that day, that his burden shall be taken away from off thy shoulder, and his yoke from off thy neck, and the yoke shall be destroyed because of the anointing.

Isaiah 10:27 KJV

Have you ever wondered why you can't shake that anxiety, no matter how many times you pray and renew your mind? You've been prayed for so many times, but that sickness still remains. You surround yourself with Spirit-filled people, you only listen to worship music, you read the Bible for hours, but you still experience depression and can't ever seem to feel joy. You try so hard to break that addiction. You truly don't want to do drugs, watch porn, sleep around, but it's as though a force stronger than you is forcing you to do these things. All the while, you feel consumed with guilt and shame, thinking, *It's just my weakness that makes it so hard for me to change.* The truth is, you need God's anointing to destroy these "yokes."

The anointing is the measure of God's power that He puts in a vessel. This power destroys yokes. Oxen have a yoke on their necks, which is connected to a heavy load of passengers or goods. It is a heavy burden placed upon them, and they are stuck in that yoke until someone releases them from it. In the spiritual realm, yokes are demonic oppression (demons) that bind you. They cannot be removed through your own effort alone, such as getting counseling, taking medicine, praying, fasting or reading the Bible. Only the anointing can destroy these yokes.

## WHERE IS THE ANOINTING FOUND?

The anointing is found in human vessels. God chooses vessels to put His anointing in. All the yoke-destroying miracles we see throughout the Bible happen through human vessels. The signs and wonders that led to the yoke of slavery being destroyed off the Israelites happened through Moses. It wasn't God doing miracles from the sky; it was God doing them through Moses.

Elisha's anointing was so powerful that a dead man came alive when his body touched Elisha's bones (see 2 Kings 13:20–21). Paul's anointing was so extraordinary and unusual that when sick or demon-possessed people touched the handkerchiefs that had touched his skin, they would immediately be healed (see Acts 19:11–12). Notice how it was a handkerchief that had specifically touched Paul, an anointed vessel, that destroyed the yokes. Peter also carried a strong anointing where demons were cast out and the sick were healed just by being near his presence and having the touch of his shadow fall on them when he passed by (see Acts 5:14–16). The anointing has a location! It is found in human vessels.

There is a difference between receiving the Holy Spirit at salvation and receiving the anointing. Everyone who believes in Jesus receives the Holy Spirit. But not everyone who has the Holy Spirit receives the anointing. The anointing is the Holy

Spirit, but it is a specific measure of the Holy Spirit moving in power through a human vessel.

When you give your life to Jesus, the Holy Spirit comes and lives in you. You can now hear from God and commune with Him. The baptism of the Holy Spirit goes beyond that. It is when the Holy Spirit comes upon you the way we see happen in the book of Acts: "But you will receive power when the Holy Spirit comes on you" (Acts 1:8; see also Acts 8:14–17; 10:44–47). Now you are activated and ready to walk in the power of God. Yet God has to first trust you before He can give you the measure of His power.

With the baptism of the Holy Spirit, you can speak in tongues, which is communing directly with the Holy Spirit and speaking God's will, as well as edifying your spirit man (pushing your flesh down and building up your spirit). The baptism of the Holy Spirit also empowers you to live surrendered to God and fills you with fire and passion for Him and His Kingdom.

People can still be prideful, however, even with the baptism of the Holy Spirit. They can be disobedient to God and still pray in tongues. Spirit-filled people can grieve the Holy Spirit and be like the Israelites in the wilderness, wandering forever and dying before they reach the promised land of walking in anointing. Carrying the anointing is something different than just having the Holy Spirit and praying in tongues. There is a cost to the anointing. Anointing comes as God inspects your heart and finds you humble. Anointing comes when God can see that you have a heart like David's—a heart after His heart, His desires and His will, rather than your own dreams, agenda, status and ego.

Anointing is God's true power. When misused, it can lead many away from God. When misused, it can do a lot of damage to the Kingdom of God and advance the devil's kingdom. That is why God is very careful with releasing His anointing. The vessel must be trustworthy. The heart has to be right.

## THE AUTHORITY OF THE ANOINTING

A yoke is a demonic chain in the spiritual realm. To remove these, you have to have the authority to remove them. You can't pray any which way. They will not be lifted unless you truly have the authority to lift them.

When the disciples returned from casting out demons for the first time, Jesus said, "I have given you authority over all the power of the enemy" (Luke 10:19 NLT). In other words, Jesus was saying, "Yes, this is why the demons obeyed you. This is why you were able to remove the yokes. Because I have given you authority to remove those demonic yokes. I have given you authority over those demons. They must obey."

What many people don't realize is that many sicknesses, disorders and oppression like addiction, anxiety, depression, suicidal thoughts and night terrors are actually demonic, meaning a demonic spirit is causing these afflictions. People try to pray the afflictions away, saying, *God, take it away! God, heal me!* People take medicine and go through counseling, but the problem still remains. Maybe the problem is numbed or medicated, but deep down it is still there, because the root of the symptom is a demonic spirit.

To get rid of a demonic spirit, you must have authority over that spirit and execute that authority properly. Praying any old way won't do it. You can't simply pray *God, take it away!* when Jesus told you "I've given *you* authority over the demons; *you* cast them out" (by God's power in you). To cast out means to take action and authority over the demon.

## HOW SPIRITUAL AUTHORITY WORKS

Let's look at how authority works in the spirit realm. You have the choice to give God authority over your life in all situations (meaning you say yes to His will), or to give the enemy authority over your life (meaning you say yes to the devil's will). "The thief does not come except to steal, and to kill, and to destroy. I have come that they may have life, and that they may have it more abundantly" (John 10:10 NKJV). The way the devil is able to accomplish stealing, killing and destroying in a person's life is when that person accepts the devil's will.

When Jesus shed His blood on the cross, and even before going on the cross, He was purchasing complete abundant life for you as your inheritance. By His stripes you are healed (see Acts 26:17–18; Isaiah 53:5). Healing is now your inheritance. In fact, *abundant* health is now your inheritance. Abundant life means abundance in every area—in your mind, in your body, in your relationships, in your finances.

As Christians, we need to understand that abundant life is our inheritance. We should view lack in our life as something that cannot stay and does not belong to us, because we know what our inheritance is. We should view many sicknesses, oppression, poverty, etc. as lies of the devil. He brings you a lie and tries to get you to believe that it's the truth. For example, because you feel anxiety and the doctor has diagnosed you as having anxiety, the devil tells you that anxiety is your portion. When you accept this as your portion and reality, in the spiritual realm what you're doing is actually accepting the devil's will in your life, which is the action of handing over your authority to the devil. Instead, you should take authority over every lie of the devil in your life.

The Bible says to "take every thought captive" to Christ (2 Corinthians 10:5). So when you're feeling anxious, you should identify that anxious thought as a lie from the devil. "Submit yourselves, then, to God. Resist the devil, and he will flee from you" (James 4:7). You can say aloud, "I reject that lie of anxiety/ depression/rage/sickness/suicidal thoughts/nightmares." And then declare Scripture aloud that speaks of God's will for your life. If you're feeling anxious, you should speak aloud from the

Scriptures, "God did not give me a spirit of fear, but of power, love, and a sound mind. I have perfect peace. Jesus has given this to me. It is my inheritance. Fear is not allowed to be in me. Any lie of fear must go" (see 2 Timothy 1:7; Isaiah 26:3). In the spiritual realm, this is the act of taking authority over the devil.

God has given you authority over all the earth (see Genesis 1:26–28). He wants you to walk in authority by bringing His will to this earth. So you are constantly saying, *Thy will be done. King Jesus, I use the authority you've given me to bring your will to this earth and in my life.*

As long as you are serious about constantly taking authority over the enemy's schemes in your life, he must defer to you every time. If you've never used the authority God has given you before, it's time to start. If you take this seriously, you will see drastic transformation in your life immediately. The devil has tried hard to keep this truth hidden from believers. Many in the Body of Christ today have no idea that they actually have authority over the issues the devil has brought on in their lives, and that they can access the full abundant life Jesus gives, if they will just use the authority they've been given.

Every believer has been given authority over the devil's attacks in his or her personal life, and every believer is given a measure of authority over the devil's work in other people's lives (depending on his or her calling and heart). Jesus said, "I have given you authority to trample on snakes and scorpions and to overcome all the power of the enemy; nothing will harm you" (Luke 10:19). It was this authority given to the disciples that made the demons leave!

The anointing God puts in a human vessel also contains authority. When demons see your anointing, they also see your authority. They see that the anointing upon you has the authority to destroy yokes. The more anointing/authority, the more demons are cast out, the higher the level of the demons cast out (such as principalities), and the quicker, with less effort, they are cast out. What makes demons leave is first, when they see that anointing/authority is in a vessel; second, when they see that the vessel knows the authority he or she has; and third, when they see that the vessel knows how to use that authority properly.

Many sicknesses actually have a demonic root. Some sicknesses are actually a spirit (demon) of infirmity. Since a demon is at the root of such sicknesses, a vessel with authority must use that authority to command the demon of infirmity to leave. Some months ago, I was in a large city, ministering at a "Revival Is Now" event. During the mass deliverance corporate prayer at the end of service, I spoke out "I command the spirit of infirmity to leave." A woman who had a chronic illness and who was deaf because of it immediately fell to the ground and testified that as she fell, she felt something leave her. As soon as it left, her ears opened. She was wearing hearing aids, and suddenly everything was too loud because she had regained her hearing and no longer needed them! She has since testified that she hears perfectly now.

Simply saying "I pray that you are healed" to her didn't work in that case. For that sickness to leave, there needed to be a vessel who carried authority to command the spirit of infirmity to leave. This is a major reason why we see that *all* sicknesses were healed in the Acts Church, but today we only see some healed, or few. Many in the Body of Christ don't know that we have to take authority over many afflictions because they actually come from demonic roots, and casting out the demons is what makes the demons, and therefore the afflictions, go.

Jesus told us to cast out demons. That's a command. That's an action. He didn't say, "Pray that the demons will leave; pray that the Father in heaven will make the demons go." It is Jesus' power that makes the demons go, but it is our job, which He gave us to do, to take authority over the demons and cast them out.

## DIFFERENT LEVELS OF THE ANOINTING

There are different levels of the anointing. It is God's will for every believer to carry the anointing, but the anointing in each believer will look different, according to God's perfect plan and purposes.

There are also different levels of demonic powers in the spiritual realm: "For we do not wrestle against flesh and blood, but against principalities, against powers, against the rulers of the darkness of this age, against spiritual hosts of wickedness in the heavenly places" (Ephesians 6:12 NKJV). This verse is actually speaking of the different levels. For example, principalities mean "princes" of their spiritual territory. Principalities are the highest level of demonic power. In the same way, in the Kingdom of God there are different levels of anointing. Principalities can only be cast out with high levels of anointing.

This is one reason why a person who is ministering might see some demons cast out of people when he or she prays, while other higher-level demons seem more stubborn about leaving. The spiritual insights I will share with you in this book will help you receive higher levels of anointing to deal with higher-level demons, and you will learn the solutions for seeing every person set free.

The Bible clearly shows us that there are different levels of anointing. Paul was doing "extraordinary" miracles, which shows us that he carried a higher level, a greater anointing than most people: "God did extraordinary miracles through Paul, so that even handkerchiefs and aprons that had touched him were taken to the sick, and their illnesses were cured and the evil spirits left them" (Acts 19:11–12). Also according to this verse, he wasn't having to spend hours casting out demons; many times he wasn't even having to say a word to cast them out. The anointing was so strong in him that when a handkerchief that had touched Paul touched a person with demons, the demons had to leave!

We also see a high level of anointing operating in the apostle Peter:

> Nevertheless, more and more men and women believed in the Lord and were added to their number. As a result, people brought the sick into the streets and laid them on beds and mats so that at least Peter's shadow might fall on some of them as he passed by. Crowds gathered also from the towns around Jerusalem, bringing their sick and those tormented by impure spirits, and all of them were healed.
>
> Acts 5:14–16

Wait a second, *all of them were healed?* Are we hearing any church report in these days we live in that *all* of the sick and demon oppressed who come to a church are healed? The apostle Peter must have been walking in a higher level of anointing than what we see today, for the most part. If all were healed, that means even the principalities had to leave. There was an ease with Peter as well, in which the demons fled and the sick were healed. Just his shadow touching the people healed them! Like Paul, many times Peter didn't even have to say a word. People were quickly healed and set free with ease, because of the higher-level anointing.

It is God's will for this same anointing that the apostles Peter and Paul walked in to be accessed today! Jesus made us this promise: "Anyone who believes in me will do the same works I have done, and even greater works" (John 14:12 NLT). Before He returns, the Bride has to be ready. The Bride has to be blameless, spotless and pure. The Body of Christ has to first look like the Acts Church, and then go from glory to glory and do "even greater works." *Revival Is Now*, and God is now pouring out His anointing (even the extraordinary anointing) on His

Church. It is God's will for every believer to walk in His anointing, and it is time now that true believers with pure, humble, childlike hearts receive and walk in it.

We are in a *Kingdom* of God. Webster defines *kingdom* as "a politically organized community or major territorial unit having a monarchical form of government headed by a king or queen."* In the Kingdom of God, Jesus is King, and He has a government (the Body of Christ) to which He has given authority. We bring God's will and the ideals of His Kingdom to this earth as we walk in our positions of authority in the Kingdom.

There are different levels of authority/anointing in the Kingdom of God, just as there are different positions and levels of authority in an earthly kingdom. The level of authority/anointing people receive is based on their specific calling and their heart. You must have a trustworthy heart to receive a high level of anointing. Then it is also simply according to God's plan which level of anointing He wants to distribute for His own purposes. Those in the five-fold ministry operate in the highest level of anointing because they are the ones called to equip and impart to the Body of Christ (see Ephesians 4:11–16). Where you receive from must be greater than what you already have, and you can eventually walk in a higher level of anointing than even those who equip you and impart to you, if that is God's will. We see this in Elisha's story, as Elisha received a double portion of anointing from his spiritual father, Elijah.

We are all called to heal the sick and cast out demons, but it will look different depending on your specific calling. The Church is where the higher-level demons are cast out and the higher-level miracles happen, for the most part, because that's where high levels of anointing are usually carried. People would

*_Merriam-Webster_, s.v. "kingdom," accessed December 5, 2022, https://www.merriam-webster.com/dictionary/kingdom.

bring the sick and demon possessed under the apostle Peter's shadow, who was a leader in the Church, because they knew he carried such a high level of anointing that even the highest-level demons had to obey.

Every believer is called to walk in the anointing, but not everyone may be called to deal with principalities. In the Body of Christ, the correct order for walking in authority and seeing the most effective miracles is this: Each believer is to walk in his or her own domain of authority, and also to bring people under "the apostle Peter's shadow" of today, so to speak. For example, let's say you encounter someone throughout your day who is talking about having dark, suicidal thoughts. If the person is open to prayer and has come to you, this is within your domain of authority. Pray for that person. Take authority over those demonic spirits in him or her. Declare that those suicidal thoughts must go!

This is how our Christian life should be. Whenever you encounter the works of the devil in your domain, take authority over them and release the anointing God has given you. It will look different for every believer, but you are truly called to carry God's power. When you speak or pray, your words will carry power and bring healing and freedom! God wants you to be a vessel of His power so that people can truly meet Him and have a tangible encounter with Him through you.

In modern times, anointing is rare. It can appear as though only a few ministers (in comparison to how many there are in the world) carry this unique anointing to walk in miracles. It was never God's will for just a couple of people to carry the anointing, however. It is His will for all believers to walk in His power:

> And these signs shall follow them that believe; in my name shall they cast out devils; they shall speak with new tongues; they shall take up serpents; and if they drink any deadly thing, it

shall not hurt them; they shall lay hands on the sick, and they shall recover.

Mark 16:17–18 KJV

*All* who believe! Not just a few ministers with big platforms. *All* who believe! It is God's will for you to pray for the sick and for His power to flow through you and heal them. It is God's will for you to walk in authority and cast out demons. It is God's will for you to speak prophetically and encourage and edify the Body of Christ. It is God's will for you to be a vessel that He moves through to baptize people in the Holy Spirit. Imagine how different the world would be today if every believer were a vessel of God's power!

# 2

# Why We Need the Anointing

My message and my preaching were not with wise and persuasive words, but with a demonstration of the Spirit's power, so that your faith might not rest on human wisdom, but on God's power.

1 Corinthians 2:4-5

I grew up in a Christian home, and I remember first saying the "Sinner's Prayer" at four years old in my living room. I was sitting on the couch with my mom, and my dad was in the recliner. That's literally my earliest memory! I don't have a single memory of not believing in Jesus.

In my childhood through college years, however, my faith rested on man's words and not on God's power. Meaning, I never had an actual encounter with God. I never felt His Spirit or witnessed a move of the Spirit. I never witnessed His power move upon people and heal or deliver them. I just believed in Jesus. But my belief was just because I believed my parents; I believed what I was taught.

I believed in the Bible because I was taught to believe in it. I never doubted a day in my life the reality of Jesus, or doubted the fact that He loved me and had good plans for me. But I didn't feel as if I really knew Jesus as a best friend, or knew God as a Father. I guess you could compare it to how children believe in Santa. It felt like that. A belief, but not a knowing. A belief in God, whom I did not personally know.

## SURRENDER BASED ON GOD'S POWER

True surrender to God happens only when you really meet Him and know Him. When you know deep down His love for you and move from a *belief* to a *knowing*. How can you devote your life to one you're not in love with? I loved Jesus, but I wasn't in love with Him, because I hadn't really met Him. Therefore, I lived a lukewarm Christian life in high school and college.

I knew I always felt a special love for God that was different from other people. I always went to Bible study and church, and I never missed a midweek or Sunday service in college. But I still lived with one foot in the world. I would go to parties. I would drink. I would want attention from guys. I wouldn't read the Bible or spend personal time with Jesus in prayer. I always desired to surrender because I believed it was the right thing to do. But for years, I was stuck. For years, I set out to open the Bible and it never happened. I felt guilt and shame for this reason. I would say the Sinner's Prayer every Sunday and raise my hand at the altar call week after week, year after year, but nothing was changing on the inside. There was no surrender from the heart.

Much of the preaching I heard carried no power, but instead was full of "wise and persuasive words." The sermons were entertaining, philosophical and persuasive. It was man's effort to get you to believe in God. Week after week, many hands were raised and they were counted in a tally and celebrated. But I wonder how many hands raised were true lives saved, true lives surrendered.

When I was 24, I found this hunger in me for more of God that just started and kept growing. Hunger for God is a beautiful thing, because the hunger leads you to seek more of Him. And as the Bible says, "You will seek me and find me when you seek me with all your heart" (Jeremiah 29:13). There is more of God to be found. But He can only be found when you seek with all your heart!

In my mid-twenties, my eyes opened up to the truth that God moves in power today. I witnessed demons being cast out, healings and other miracles for the first time. I received prophetic ministry for the first time. When I encountered God in power, it opened up my spiritual eyes like never before. His love and His nearness became so real to me.

I went from believing in God to KNOWING that He is real and always with me, knowing that He loves me intimately and knowing that His plans for me are good.

I met Jesus and fell in love with Him. The Kingdom of God is not a matter of talk, but of power. I finally met the true Jesus, who tangibly touches you with His love and encounters you with His power. His power is the supernatural manifestation of His love that destroys yokes and touches your heart in a way that it cannot be touched by any person or earthly thing. His power is His love in action—His love that moves and changes things. His power is the miraculous in your life.

Encountering God's power opened my spiritual eyes to see His love for me, His sovereignty and His majesty like never before. I suddenly had a much bigger perspective on how worthy and almighty God is. Suddenly, my heart's biggest desire was to surrender to Him. It was as if I could see that surrendering was the most important thing in the world for me to do. How dare I think I knew what was best for my life? How could I not put my whole life in God's hands and say to Him, *God, You can have my dreams, desires, plans, will, everything!* I was radically transformed that day. Instantly, the desires of the world fell away. I no longer had any desire for the lukewarm, "one foot in the world" life. I suddenly desired to read the Bible and spend personal time with God for the first time in my life. Spending alone time with God was suddenly my greatest desire.

This is why as vessels of God we minister "not with wise and persuasive words, but with a demonstration of the Spirit's power," as Paul said. My surrender was based on the power of God. For years, my faith had rested on man's words about God but had never moved my heart to truly surrender. When I finally encountered God's power, however, my faith became based on His power. That's what gave me the ability and my own heart's desire to surrender my life to Him.

I had heard thousands of altar calls and "repeat after me" Sinner's Prayers, but not one of them had moved me to give my whole life to God. It was encountering the power of God that made me give my life to Jesus. There was no altar call. There was no "repeat after me" prayer. It was wedding vows to Jesus from my own heart. The surrender was real, and it was lasting! I wasn't saved because I repeated word for word the Sinner's Prayer. I was saved because God's power touched me, so I could really see this amazing God who loved me, and I could therefore fall in love with Him.

We are all called to be ministers in one way or another—vessels of Jesus. It is God's will for every believer to be a vessel of the true Jesus who comes in power. When you minister and witness to others without God's power, how many are actually being saved? How many are actually meeting Jesus through you? Or how many are just hearing words about Him? Jesus instructed His disciples not to minister before they received the power of the Holy Spirit (see Acts 1:4). He instructed this because He wanted His disciples to truly carry Him inside themselves so people could actually have encounters with God through them, not just hear about Him.

## THE ANOINTING DESTROYS THE DEVIL'S KINGDOM

We need the anointing to destroy the devil's kingdom. When you read the gospels and look at the ministry of Jesus, you will find out how important it was to Him that God's children be healed and delivered. When you study His ministry, you find that healing the sick, casting out demons, and doing miracles, signs and wonders always accompanied His preaching. Those things were His demonstration of love to His people. If a parent sees his or her child suffering pain, the most important thing in the world to that parent is to relieve the child's suffering. Jesus paid the price for God's children to be healed by His stripes (see Isaiah 53:5) and be delivered from the devil's yokes. Jesus wants us to be healed and free, period!

So many Christians don't have their eyes fully open to God's love because they truly don't *know* that Jesus' love is so powerful that whenever a child of God is sick or oppressed, He absolutely wants that person healed and free. And He will do it! Before my spiritual eyes opened to see that God was miraculously healing and delivering people today, my understanding of His love was limited. When I saw so many Christians struggling with oppression and sickness, I didn't understand why.

One day, I went to the church of my spiritual father, Prophet Dr. GeorDavie, and there I witnessed mass deliverance for the first time. I saw demon after demon speak out of person after person, revealing the ways that they were trying to torture and kill these people. It opened my eyes like never before to see how evil the devil is and also how hard at work he is to torment so many people. And then the next moment, I saw the authority of Christ in my spiritual father like I had never seen demonstrated. I saw him get so serious with those demons and sternly command them to leave person after person. And as he commanded the demons, they all left, and fast!

In that moment, my eyes opened up like never before to see how much God really does love His children, and how it really is His will to heal and deliver every single one. In that moment, it was as if I fully understood that Jesus loves His children so much that He wants freedom and healing for them *all*. But it is up to us as vessels to be humble and be ones who can actually be trusted with the anointing. It is up to us to pay whatever cost necessary to receive the anointing. A great knowing came over me in that moment: *The way to receive the anointing is a narrow road.*

We cannot manipulate God and receive the anointing our own way. It has to be God's way. God is waiting to heal and deliver every one of His children. He is waiting on those in the Body of Christ to humble themselves and be vessels He can trust to pour out His anointing on.

When your eyes have opened up to see that God's anointing is here and available, how can you go back to your lukewarm Christian life? You see everyone differently. You see people with all this oppression, and it breaks your heart to know that they are in a church where the pastor is embarrassed about the move of the Holy Spirit and has closed the door for the Spirit to move in power and free people. *What are we doing without the anointing?* Jesus told us to heal the sick and cast out demons. We cannot ignore this commission any longer. We cannot preach sermon after sermon while demons stay hiding in the people we're preaching to, laughing at us. Without the anointing, that's precisely what is happening in churches all over. Demons comfortably remain, and people remain in bondage.

We have a responsibility as the Body of Christ to present the full Gospel to the world: Jesus has come to heal you, deliver you, and give you abundant life, in addition to removing your sins, making a way for you to live eternally in heaven, and tearing the veil so you can have intimacy with God now. For so long, much of the Church has been preaching only a partial Gospel, but leaving out the fact that Jesus endured scourging for us to be healed and delivered here and now. "My people are destroyed for lack of knowledge" (Hosea 4:6 KJV). So many believers are being destroyed by the devil's yokes simply because they've never been given this basic knowledge of the Gospel: *Jesus paid a price for your healing and freedom!*

The demons have hidden in the Church far too long. It's time we stop trying to fix spiritual problems with worldly solutions. People have anxiety and their church sends them to a counselor or a doctor to give them medicine, when what they really need is deliverance from a spirit of anxiety. A teen testified recently that she was delivered from constant suicidal thoughts at a "Revival Is Now" event in another city. She said that from that day on, the suicidal thoughts completely left! People with an addiction don't need rehab; they need deliverance. A different woman recently testified that when she went to a previous "Revival Is Now" event in another state, God delivered her from a decades-long cigarette addiction. She tried to smoke a few days after the event, and the cigarette repulsed her!

How are we ministering without the anointing? We have a responsibility to help God's people by His power and destroy the devil's yokes in their lives. As I mentioned earlier, Jesus told the disciples that they should not even go out to minister before they received the power of His Spirit (see Luke 24:49).

When your eyes have opened up to see that God's anointing is available here on this earth now, you have a great responsibility to share this truth with as many people as possible and to be a servant of God who truly advances His Kingdom. "For the Kingdom of God is not a matter of talk but of power" (1 Corinthians 4:20).

This is urgent—like an emergency! For instance, so many people are tormented by a suicidal spirit. This is life or death!

Simply share with as many people as possible that "Jesus can free you! I've seen it done! It has happened to me!" Your words can ignite faith in people who are oppressed, and they can be freed instantly with just a touch of the anointing. Countless testimonies have come in from people who have received deliverance and healing just by watching the services at 5F Church, or the "Revival Is Now" services (my livestreams). Uncountable testimonies have come in about people who have received deliverance even by watching a one-minute video of another person being delivered or testifying about deliverance.

It's time to spread this Good News—the full Good News! *The full Gospel!* God is moving in power, just as He did in the Acts Church. He is healing every sickness and casting out every demon. *Revival Is Now.* He has chosen this time in history to release the anointing that we have longed for and prayed for, for so many years. It's time to get serious about spreading this Good News far and wide, and get serious about becoming a vessel whom God can entrust with the anointing so He can save, heal and deliver the most people possible.

# 3

# The Cost of the Anointing

Then Jesus said to his disciples, "Whoever wants to be my disciple must deny themselves and take up their cross and follow me."

Matthew 16:24

On the day I cast out my first demon, I hadn't set out to do that. Even when I started praying for the woman involved, I didn't think, *A demon needs to be cast out of her.* To be honest, I wasn't even praying, *Lord, use me to cast out demons.* I had received the prophecy that God would use me in great power to do many miracles throughout the nations, but casting out demons wasn't the big thing I was picturing. I suppose I was just thinking about past revivals where I hadn't heard too much about demons being cast out, but had heard mostly about healings and baptisms in the Holy Spirit.

That day in the park when I was praying for this woman, the anointing inside me made the demon uncomfortable and made it start trembling. I didn't have to make it manifest. I didn't have to say, "Show yourself! Manifest!" I didn't have to do things in my own effort. What happened was that the anointing had been growing inside me for four and a half years, ever since receiving a word of prophecy and stepping into my calling as an apostle. It was as if I was pregnant with the anointing.

I had seen hints of the anointing throughout those years. In my ministry I had seen several people baptized in the Holy Spirit, and there were a handful of testimonies of people being healed, including nine children healed of HIV in Africa in 2020. As I ministered, sometimes the power of God would hit people and they would fall back. There were testimonies of spiritual transformation and growth. But it was not like the anointing I am seeing today, where tons of demons are manifesting and coming out of many people at the same time and many miracles are happening at every service.

That day in the park, March 21, 2021, before the demons began to tremble under my ministry, I spoke these words firmly over the woman: "Those attacks against you keeping you from receiving from God—I declare them to be broken off you!" She fell back with the power of God when I said those words, without my laying a hand on her. Then her whole body started to convulse.

I had never seen that happen before in my ministry. I discerned immediately that this was a demon manifesting. As I told you in the introduction, the demon spoke out of her, "I don't want her to preach." I then commanded the demon to stand up (at this point it was possessing her), and I commanded it to leave. It came out of her with such force that her body fell to the ground, as if someone had pushed her. She was free and full of peace, even sleeping for a bit. I was shocked. The demon had come out with such little physical effort. I did not yell with a loud voice; I did not put my hand on her. It was purely the anointing that made the demon go.

It is the anointing that destroys the yoke (see Isaiah 10:27 KJV). The decibel level of your voice has nothing to do with casting out a demon. It is the anointing in you, and the way in which you use the anointing and authority properly, that make demons go. When trying to cast out demons, many forget this most important fact. It is the anointing that makes demons tremble, and it is the anointing that makes them leave a person. It is the power of Jesus—the anointing—that is one hundred percent the force that makes a demon go. We vessels don't have even one percent power. We are simply vessels for the anointing to flow through. If you really want to cast out demons and walk in signs, wonders and miracles, you need to be a vessel in whom God can put the anointing. This is the foundation and core of how to walk in miracles.

So the questions to ask are not, *How can I do miracles? How can I cast out demons?* Rather, the question is, *How can I access the anointing?* The anointing power of Jesus does the miracles—not you. How do you get this anointing? Many people think it comes when you have fasted and prayed a certain number of times. But God is not keeping a tally of religious rituals. You cannot earn or buy the anointing through religious rituals or practices. Accessing the anointing is very simple, although the spirit of religion has made it complicated.

*Here is the secret to accessing the anointing: You have to be a trustworthy vessel.* God has to see that your heart can be trusted. He has to test your heart, test your surrender, test your obedience and find that you have proven trustworthy. Many people don't make it past these tests because their selfish ambition, pride and lack of surrender get in the way. God looks at the heart. He knows your motives.

This anointing is real power. When you walk in the anointing, you become a representative of God, with a spotlight on you. You better be representing God rightly, and you better be stewarding the anointing correctly, or you can lead souls away from Him. This is very serious. God does not treat distributing the anointing casually; He is extremely serious about it. It's not good enough to say, *Lord, give me your anointing so I can cast out demons and heal the sick! I yearn for this!* Faith without works is dead (see James 2:17). Your faith must be proven by your actions.

## A TRUSTWORTHY VESSEL'S SURRENDER

The first quality God is looking for when He searches for a trustworthy vessel is *complete surrender*. Before 2016, I was a Christian but I was not yet surrendered. I lived with one foot in the world, where I would still follow some of my own desires instead of God's will. About one month after I encountered the power of God, however, I was baptized in the Holy Spirit. In that moment, my spiritual eyes opened to see God's love, worthiness and majesty like never before. My whole being yearned to surrender to Him. It was as though that was the only thing I wanted. It was the only thing that made sense in the world!

I surrendered completely to God the day I was baptized in the Holy Spirit, January 7, 2016, six days after my twenty-fifth birthday. I remember telling God, *You can take my dreams, even!* Even if He wanted to send me to a private island by myself, He could. I felt this desperation to surrender literally everything. To surrender my dreams was no small thing, because my dreams were so special to me. But on that day, I really handed them over to God and gave Him permission to do whatever He wanted with my life.

Little did I know that in nine months would come the test of those words I had spoken to God. In September 2016, I attended a conference where a prophet prophesied to me that I was called to be an apostle. To be honest, I was expectant and hopeful that he would prophesy to me about my music dreams. I really thought that being a Christian Pop/EDM (electronic dance music) singer/songwriter was my calling. The prophet said nothing about my music dream, however. He said instead, "You are an apostle of Jesus Christ, and you're called to reach the nations. I see you ministering to the masses and God doing shocking miracles through you."

I didn't want to be a minister at all! Speaking in front of people was my biggest weakness and fear. I didn't know how I would be able to do it, and I couldn't picture myself having a passion for it. Yet although I didn't desire what was prophesied, I couldn't shake the conviction I had that it was truly God speaking through this man of God. In that moment when I heard the prophecy, God immediately brought the story of Moses to my mind. Moses stuttered, yet God called him to be His mouthpiece and lead millions of people:

> Moses said to the LORD, "Pardon your servant, LORD. I have never been eloquent, neither in the past nor since you have spoken to your servant. I am slow of speech and tongue."
>
> The LORD said to him, "Who gave human beings their mouths? Who makes them deaf or mute? Who gives them sight or makes them blind? Is it not I, the LORD? Now go; I will help you speak and will teach you what to say."
>
> Exodus 4:10–12

All I wanted was to be in God's will ever since that day when I surrendered. All I wanted was to please Him. Between the combination of my main desire to be in His will, and God reminding me of Moses' story for encouragement, I was able to quickly and easily say yes. I have never felt so uncertain about the future in my entire life, however. I thought, *How on earth will I be able to preach and minister to people?!* I couldn't picture it, but I knew with God nothing is impossible. I knew He would give me the ability. I also couldn't picture myself having a heart to minister, but I knew that if God had called me to do this, He would definitely mold my heart to be like His about it. I trusted Him. I thought, *If He created me for this, then He definitely will give me the heart for it!*

I know that if I hadn't said yes to God that day, I would not be where I am today. I would not be a vessel of God's anointing. You can't receive anointing in your own way, in your comfort zone. It doesn't work to say, *Well, God, actually how about you anoint me to sing? That's what I want to do. So how about you give me anointing, and as I sing, miracles will happen?*

We cannot bargain with God or manipulate Him. Anointing will never come to you in that way. When God calls you to carry the anointing, there will be a test of your surrender—a great test! In many cases, it will be as extreme for you as it was for me, where you literally have to lay aside your dreams and say yes to doing something you have no desire to do. That's an extreme test of surrender. How can God test your surrender when there is nothing to lose?

Moses had no desire to do what God called him to do. He was content being a shepherd and living a good distance away from the Israelites. They reminded him of his past, where he had murdered a man, and where for his whole childhood he had been lied to about his heritage. But God called him to do what he didn't dream or desire to do.

Mary had her own dreams and plans for living a simple life married to Joseph and having his children, the typical dreams of a Hebrew woman in those days. She had to abandon those dreams to obey God in the difficult thing He was calling her to do, carrying the Messiah when no one understood it and people shunned her.

All of Jesus' disciples had their own plans for their lives before they met Him. They definitely were not planning to be anointed vessels of God. Many were fishermen, including Peter. Matthew was a tax collector. Simon was a Zealot attempting to overthrow the Roman government. None of these guys were like, *I want to be an anointed minister of God.* God chooses the same kind of people today. For the most part, the ones He chooses to anoint are those who had no plans to be used so powerfully. There are a couple of reasons why God chooses these types of people: (1) Their yes requires a greater surrender. The greater the calling, the greater the surrender/the cost; (2) He chooses the foolish things to confound the wise: "But God chose the foolish things of the world to shame the wise; God chose the weak things of the world to shame the strong" (1 Corinthians 1:27).

Why does God choose the foolish things? So that no one may boast: "God chose the lowly things of this world and the despised things—and the things that are not—to nullify the things that are, so that no one may boast before him" (1 Corinthians 1:28–29). So that the ones chosen may stay in continual awe that God would choose them for something they couldn't dream of doing. People chosen this way are not the types who feel entitled, who lack humility or who don't see their great need for God to do anything. Instead, they are the types who ask, *Why me, God? You really want to use me? Who am I to have this honor of being used by you in such a great way?*

To receive anointing from God, you must lay down everything. There is a great cost to carrying the anointing, and the cost is your entire life—your dreams, your desires, your preferences, your reputation. The cost of the anointing is great because there is actually more and more that God will ask you to surrender as time goes on. When you thought you had surrendered all, God will ask you to surrender even more.

When God lifts you and blesses you, there is then more to surrender. For example, when you don't have much money, there is less to surrender to God. But when God blesses you financially so much, He will ask you to surrender the abundance of finances you now have. Giving $10 to God when that's all you have is indeed giving God a lot and is definitely surrendering. But when God asks you to give $100,000 when $100,000 is what you have, this is a different level of surrender in your finances.

Ever since August 2021, I have been traveling almost every week to minister in different states and countries. I come back every Saturday to minister in Los Angeles on Sundays. My schedule has never been so busy. I am flying two days a week, usually very early in the morning, with little sleep. I once had free time, but now my time is mostly spent serving God and doing His work. In this season, there is very little time for me to go do something fun or just "hang out." When I minister in different cities and countries, I usually don't have time to see any of the places I'm in. I am so grateful that this is my life, however, because pleasing God is my biggest passion and I am living in promises fulfilled. I have never been so happy in my entire life!

At the same time, this season has required a greater surrender than the previous season. God is asking for more of my time and energy, and I'm giving it to Him. I have also faced more persecution than ever before in my life. This also comes with a greater surrender. God is asking me to be more patient than ever before, be more loving and be more careful only to speak life. It is a new level of surrender for me only to praise God and never complain when the level of persecution is higher than ever; to keep my eyes focused on Jesus and not get consumed with negative things people are saying against me; to keep moving forward, doing the work of God with joy and with passion, even when I'm being persecuted and emotionally abused. It can be hurtful and taxing, and you sometimes just want a breather, but God is asking you to keep going.

When God first calls you, that begins the surrender. But it is just the beginning. It is the first cost. Yet it is a lifetime of deeper levels of surrender and higher costs. God lifts the humble. The lower you go, with more surrender and paying the price spiritually, the higher God lifts you for His glory.

## SACRIFICIAL LOVE FOR OTHERS

In the Bible, it's very clear why David was specifically chosen to be the anointed king. God removes the present king, Saul, and appoints a new king, testifying about him, "I have found David son of Jesse, a man after my own heart; he will do everything I want him to do" (Acts 13:22). David was chosen because he had a heart after God's heart. That means he put God's desires before his own. His heart was, *What makes God happy? What does God want? What are God's dreams?*

A heart after God's own heart truly puts God's desires before its own. A heart after God's heart wants to please God more than anything. What grieves this heart most is to see the Holy Spirit grieved, or to do something that would hurt God. This heart takes obedience to God so seriously that every word and action comes with the intention to please Him.

God's biggest passion is His people. That is God's whole heart. He wants to see His children's eyes open up to how much He loves them. He wants the devil's works destroyed in their lives. He wants His children healed and delivered. He wants them to know His compassion, mercy and forgiveness. He wants them to know His love so well that they are overflowing with it and become His vessels so more people can be saved and know His love, too.

Your purpose on this earth is to be a vessel of God to reach those who are lost, so they will encounter God's love through you. God chooses to use humans as vessels to move through. The more you are a great vessel of God's love, the more people will encounter His love and be saved. Many people wonder, *What is my purpose?* Well, this is it! It is simple: *Be the best vessel of God you can be.* Everything else comes second. The specific ways you are to be a vessel of God will come in God's perfect timing.

Serving God is this: being a vessel of God, representing Him to the world and allowing His love and power to flow through you. It is denying yourself and surrendering all, so that your carnal nature dies and you are transformed into God's image. It is where you are only loving others and never hurting them. As Jesus told us,

> You have heard that it was said, "Love your neighbor and hate your enemy." But I tell you, love your enemies and pray for those who persecute you, that you may be children of your Father in heaven.
>
> Matthew 5:43–45

This is where many believers fall short of passing the "trustworthy heart" test to carry the anointing. To be like Jesus means loving everyone, not just those whom you like and who are nice to you, but your enemies as well!

We are called to love those who persecute us and do evil things to us. What does this love look like? It does not mean that you want to be best friends with your persecutors, or even that you have a loving feeling toward those who do bad things to you. Loving your enemies looks like refusing to take an eye for eye. Jesus also told us,

> You have heard that it was said, "Eye for eye, and tooth for tooth." But I tell you, do not resist an evil person. If anyone slaps you on the right cheek, turn to them the other cheek also.
>
> Matthew 5:38–39

We need to look at people with the eyes of Jesus. I will never forget the day God opened up my spiritual eyes so I would be able to love other people with the love of Christ, including my enemies. I was at a deliverance service at my spiritual father's church. I witnessed mass deliverance that day for the first time in my life. I witnessed demons tremble in person after person. Many times, the demons would speak about what they were doing to the people—such evil things. This opened my eyes like never before to how evil the devil is. I never quite comprehended before that the devil was really after so many people's lives, and that so many were in actual bondage. I had never experienced demonic torment, so I had never quite realized how much other people were suffering as they were caught in the chains of demons.

One demon described all the ways he was trying to kill a woman, including sending a rock down her throat. I was shocked that day as my eyes opened up to the devil's work in many people's lives. I realized that many people are the way they are because they're in bondage. Many people don't want to be addicted, but they have a demon of addiction and they are in bondage to it. Many people don't want to have angry outbursts and be mean to others, but they have a demon of rage. Many people's faults, which make us dislike them or even feel that they're our enemies, are actually the result of demonic oppression. It's not that a person is mean or selfish and won't stop his or her addiction. It's that the person just needs freedom!

I then saw my spiritual father, full of the power of God, cast out demon after demon in a quick instant. I could see before my eyes how tortured people were by the devil, and then I could see the triumph of Jesus. Wow, how amazing His love is! He sees people in bondage, and He comes and just frees them in an instant because He loves them. His compassion and love move Him to deliver His people.

When I came home from that trip to my spiritual father's church, I was able to see people with God's love like never before. From then on, every time someone did something mean to me, I was able to see what was going on in the spiritual realm. Instead of getting offended that the person was mean when I had done nothing wrong, I would realize, *The devil is really attacking this person and has him (or her) in chains.*

*This person needs freedom! I want this person to be free and to encounter God's love!*

If you really know God's love, His love will be overflowing out of you. If you really know His love, that's when you can love other people well. So every time I would encounter someone who was mean to me or seemed like my enemy, I would discipline myself spiritually to see the person with Jesus' eyes. My heart would be for him or her to become free and encounter God's love. This is how you love your enemies: *See them with God's eyes and only speak life over them; never speak badly about them.*

Jesus gave us the best example of how to love our enemies. The Pharisees accused Him of many things, all of which were lies. They even went as far as to accuse Him of using demonic power to cast out demons: "But when the Pharisees heard this, they said, 'It is only by Beelzebul, the prince of demons, that this fellow drives out demons'" (Matthew 12:24). Jesus didn't stop His ministry to start an eye-for-an-eye campaign against the Pharisees. He didn't waste time preaching whole sermons defending Himself and speaking bad things about the Pharisees. He never cursed them. He wouldn't put the Pharisees' individual names on blast and say, "This person is so evil." Instead, Jesus stayed focused on His mission to minister to people and reveal His love to them. Even when He was on the cross, He demonstrated love to His enemies:

> When they came to the place called the Skull, they crucified him there, along with the criminals—one on his right, the other on his left. Jesus said, "Father, forgive them, for they do not know what they are doing."
>
> Luke 23:33–34

Do you see Jesus' amazing heart of compassion? He knew His enemies were spiritually blind, so that was why they were being so mean to Him. They were lost. He didn't take offense and wish ill toward them. Every person on this earth is God's child, whom He has created and loves. He wants every one of His children to be saved and know His love. To have a heart after God's heart is to see people the way Jesus saw them when they were persecuting Him.

In the story of Saul who became Paul, Saul was a Pharisee who was killing Christians. Saul was trying to destroy the work of God and was even murdering Jesus' disciples. This was a true enemy of Jesus, and an enemy of the disciples. He qualified as the hardest person to love. He did the most evil things to Jesus and the disciples directly. But look at the amazing love of Jesus, who actually desired that Saul be redeemed. He desired not only that Saul's eyes be opened so he would become a believer, but also that Saul would be used as a powerful vessel of God.

Jesus blinds Saul and speaks to him audibly: "He fell to the ground and heard a voice say to him, 'Saul, Saul, why do you persecute me?'" (Acts 9:4). In this encounter, Saul's spiritual eyes open and he realizes he has been wrong all this time. His eyes open to the amazing love of Jesus, and instantly he becomes zealous for God, and a man after God's heart. Then he wants others to be saved and know the love of Jesus.

As I mentioned in chapter 1, Paul ends up being the only apostle who is described as doing *extraordinary* miracles: "God did extraordinary miracles through Paul, so that even handkerchiefs and aprons that had touched him were taken to the sick, and their illnesses were cured and the evil spirits left them" (Acts 19:11–12). God also chose Paul to write most of the New Testament. Now, that's quite the honor Jesus chose him to have. Look at the radical compassion, forgiveness and mercy Jesus has for His people!

Imagine a modern-day Saul the persecutor. Would you be able to have the heart Jesus had toward Saul? Would you desire that a Saul-like person be transformed, and would you pray the best for that person? Would you be okay with God promoting that person higher than you in the spiritual realm, where he or she was walking in a higher level of anointing? For God's glory, Paul was lifted beyond many of the other disciples who had never killed someone or tried to stop the work of God. This is how much God wants us to forget people's pasts. And this is how much God wants us to love others and desire the best for them. He wants our heart to be, *I want this person to know God's love, be transformed and become such a powerful vessel of God!*

I see people in the Body of Christ who falsely accuse and slander servants of God, or actively try to stop them because they think a servant of God is wrong. I have had it happen to me many times. This is not the example of Jesus' love toward others. Even if you think someone is wrong, it's not your job to speak badly in public about that person, or especially to shout accusations with no evidence. God had no problem stripping the anointing from King Saul in the Old Testament and taking him down from his position, and God didn't need the help of people shouting accusations and hatred toward the king to do it. If you think someone is wrong in the ministry, your job is to love that person. If there is reason for correction, let an anointed person in a position of authority and according to God's order in the church deal with it biblically and with love (see, for example, Matthew 18:15–17).

Too many people are playing God and judging others out of hate, jealousy and selfish ambition. God calls us simply to *love*. Your enemies could be people you don't naturally like, people who are mean to you, or people who have spoken lies about you, trying to destroy you/your ministry/your career. Simply love them all. Speak only life about them all. Pray for them all. Forgive them all. Turn your cheek to them all. Allow them to say whatever evil things about you they want to say, and do whatever evil things they want to do. Allow God Himself to defend you. Allow God Himself to prepare a table for you in the presence of your enemies (see Psalm 23:5). God is a just God: "For the Lord is a God of justice. Blessed are all who wait for him!" (Isaiah 30:18) What such people sow, they will reap. But don't delight in the evil they are reaping from the evil they have sown. Instead, have a heart like Jesus had for Saul who became Paul, and desire that such people be transformed and become great vessels of God.

Many fall short of receiving the anointing because they do not take God's greatest command seriously enough:

> "Love the Lord your God with all your heart and with all your soul and with all your mind." This is the first and greatest commandment. And the second is like it: "Love your neighbor as yourself."
>
> Matthew 22:37–39

With God's help, you are truly able to love everyone. But many believers indulge too much in gossip, offense, jealousy and selfish ambition. God is watching. He sees the heart's motives. He sees careless words spoken. He sees the intent to push someone down to get ahead. This grieves Him and is a failed test in the spiritual realm. The command to love your neighbor and love your enemy is so basic and simple. But it's one of the most important, and it's forgotten among many in the Body of Christ.

If you can have God's heart for people, your heart will stand out among millions before Him. Just as He did with David, God will see your heart and raise you up. He will anoint you because you can love His people well.

For God to entrust you with the anointing, you really have to die to yourself. You have to hand over every single part of your life to God. It is a great cost, but it is worth it! The joy of being a vessel of God's power and seeing Jesus move through you to do miracles for others is a joy like no other.

# 4

# The Humility of a Childlike Heart

*Humble yourselves before the Lord, and he will lift you up.*

James 4:10

One of the biggest qualities a trustworthy heart must have to carry the anointing is humility—having a childlike heart. Shortly after the disciples returned from casting out demons for the first time, notice what Jesus said to His Father:

> At that time Jesus prayed this prayer: "O Father, Lord of heaven and earth, thank you for hiding these things from those who think themselves wise and clever, and for revealing them to the childlike. Yes, Father, it pleased you to do it this way!"
>
> Matthew 11:25-26 NLT

Jesus says that God hides "these things." What are the things? In The Passion Translation, Jesus says "you have hidden the great revelation of this authority." This means the secrets and mysteries in the Kingdom of how to access the anointing, and the revelation of how to properly execute our God-given authority. This is what makes demons leave—when one carries the anointing and authority of Christ, and when one properly executes that authority. Jesus literally says that these things are hidden "from those who are proud" (verse 25 TPT). They are *only* revealed to those who are childlike!

What does it mean to be childlike? To be childlike is to be humble. A young child rarely thinks he or she knows it all. Pride doesn't exist in a child. Children are aware that they don't know everything. They are always asking questions to learn things because they simply are aware that adults know much more than they do and they have a lot to learn. A child is teachable. When an adult teaches or corrects a child, the child doesn't get offended or say, "No, I know better than you." A child receives new things easily, with an open heart.

If you teach children something new, they don't question it. They don't have skepticism in them. The Pharisees were full of pride and skepticism. They believed they knew best and knew it all when it came to the things of God. Jesus came teaching something new, and they rejected His teachings before even listening to them, because in their minds they were the supreme godly people and no one could teach them anything new. They thought they knew exactly how to be the best godly people. They thought they knew exactly how "church" should be done.

When you are prideful, you are locking your spiritual eyes shut so you can't see the truth. Jesus says, "Though seeing, they do not see; though hearing, they do not hear or understand" (Matthew 13:13). When you close your spiritual eyes, then "these things" from Matthew 11:25—the deeper mysteries of the Kingdom—are hidden from you.

The humble and childlike don't see themselves as spiritually superior. They only see that it is God's grace they have been given, the grace to see spiritually. The humble are open to receive from God in whichever way He wants.

## GOD SPEAKS THROUGH ANOINTED VESSELS

God speaks to people in many different ways throughout the Bible. He speaks mainly through people, but also through dreams, visions, a burning bush, an audible voice and even a donkey! To be humble is to give permission for God to speak to you in any way He wants, not in your preferred way, but however He wants. These days, most people want to hear God without a human vessel involved. They want to feel as though they have heard God personally, even though when He speaks through a vessel it is just as personal, and it is the same as God speaking directly to you. Most people want to hear God's voice in a dream, a vision and on their own, without a vessel being involved.

How do you know if someone giving you a word is a true anointed vessel or not? When God has revealed to you who His anointed vessels are, you will know them by their fruits, just as you will know false prophets by their fruits:

> Watch out for false prophets. They come to you in sheep's clothing, but inwardly they are ferocious wolves. By their fruit you will recognize them. Do people pick grapes from thornbushes, or figs from thistles? Likewise, every good tree bears good fruit, but a bad tree bears bad fruit. A good tree cannot bear bad fruit, and a bad tree cannot bear good fruit. Every tree that does not bear good fruit is cut down and thrown into the fire. Thus, by their fruit you will recognize them.
>
> Matthew 7:15–20

You will see the good fruits of a true anointed vessel. I must also mention that we are called to be *childlike*, not immature and childish. Be both wise and childlike. Don't take just anybody's words as God's words. Don't take anybody's word for it who says he or she is from God, or take another person's "God says this to you" as God's words, *before* you test the person's fruits, as the Bible says to do.

Test someone's fruits with a pure heart, not looking for wrong with a critical spirit, but honestly and earnestly looking at the fruits of the person's life without bias. When you come with that heart, God will show you the truth and it will be very clear. To view things with a childlike and pure heart is the only way to hear God's voice telling you "This is Me" or "This is not Me." If you come with skepticism, it will be like the "accuser of the brethren" speaking to you, and you will have blinded yourself from hearing God's voice (see Revelation 12:10 NKJV).

God is still speaking through human vessels. One of the biggest ways He speaks today is through the vessels of prophets and prophetic voices. When He speaks through a true anointed vessel, it is really Him speaking. Many times, people don't value the words spoken by a true vessel of God, because they have a different preference for how they want to hear Him speak.

If God chooses to speak something to you through an anointed vessel, whether a word of direction, revelation or correction, you should humbly receive that word. You should not come with skepticism and the attitude, *I've never heard of that before, so I don't know* . . . You should take the word from a true vessel as a true word of God.

Many people will say "That doesn't sit right with my spirit" when they hear a new revelation from God through a true vessel, when in reality it's their pride speaking. The Bible says that the person without the Spirit does not accept the things that come from the Spirit of God, but considers them foolishness, and therefore cannot understand them because they are discerned only through the Spirit (see 1 Corinthians 2:14).

If you are prideful, you are carnal. When you hear the "things" Jesus talked about (the secrets and keys of walking in the anointing), you will call them foolish. You will say they go against the Word of God, just as the Pharisees said to Jesus. He healed a man on the Sabbath, but the Pharisees had a religious revelation of the Word where they believed it was a sin to do anything—including a miraculous work of God—on the Sabbath. By *religious* I mean that before Jesus came, the people were under the curse of the Law. The only way to be right with God was by observing the Law and following all the rituals perfectly. Jesus came to destroy the curse of the Law, and now by His grace we are saved. Now the Holy Spirit speaks God's words to us that bring true life, "for the letter kills, but the Spirit gives life" (2 Corinthians 3:6).

The Pharisees thought Jesus was going against the Word of God, when in reality He was coming with the true revelation of the Word. He was coming with new revelation, and true revelation. The Pharisees accused Jesus of not observing the Sabbath, but He came with the true revelation of the Sabbath. To keep the Sabbath means to stay in God's rest continually. It means that in everything you do, you will be resting in God as you do it, relying on Him for everything.

The whole Bible can either be read through a "religious" lens, or by the revelation of the Holy Spirit. When you are prideful and carnal, you will have a religious revelation of the Bible, and when you hear someone speaking actual revelation from the Holy Spirit, you will call it going against God's Word. God used the apostle Paul to teach most of the "spiritual things" to the early believers. Think about how much of the New Testament Paul wrote. The early Church received these revelations from God through a person, a true anointed vessel.

## BECOMING A HUMBLE DISCIPLE

Paul's disciples, his spiritual children, learned so much from God speaking through Paul. In a similar way, I have learned so much about the spiritual realm from God speaking through my spiritual father, Prophet Dr. GeorDavie of Tanzania. Because he is a true anointed prophet of God, God speaks through him. God convicted me that my spiritual father is a true vessel as I observed the good fruits in his life and ministry, and as I observed the fruits that came in my life as a result of his ministry and mentorship. Because the good fruits demonstrated the truth of his anointing, when he spoke I could therefore receive his teaching, correction, direction and prophecies as a humble child. That's how it should be when you serve and learn from an anointed mentor/spiritual parent.

My spiritual father is one of God's generals and a highly anointed prophet. Demons flee immediately in his presence, his prophecies have come to pass, presidents of African nations have sought him for spiritual advice, and he has been walking in signs, wonders and miracles for many years. He was also given the Nelson Mandela Peace Ambassador Prize because of the help and financial support he has given the people in Africa. He knows and understands many mysteries of the spiritual realm, and God has chosen him as a vessel for me to hear God through. Dr. GeorDavie carries great insight into the spiritual realm, some insight I had never heard before. As he would share the deeper things of the spiritual realm, my spirit would jump with a resounding *Yes! Aha!* When God is really speaking, your spirit and the Word of God confirm it.

The truth is, deliverance is rare today because Jesus doesn't give the revelation of the anointing and authority to just anyone. The fact that deliverance and demonstrations of God's power are so rare, yet my spiritual father was walking in the mighty power of God, humbled me to listen to his teachings and prophetic direction carefully. I came with a humble, teachable, childlike heart, hungry to learn spiritual truths from him that unlock freedom and the "more" of God. That's also how it should be when you learn from the mentor/spiritual father/mother God has chosen for you.

We must be careful we don't fall into pride. When a spiritual teaching is new to us, pride tempts us to think, *I've never heard that before, so I don't know if it's true.* Or because of pride, we think, *It has to be from* . . . (this list of famous preachers of a certain demographic, who are from a certain ministry) *for me to believe it!*

Remember whom Jesus chose to follow Him. He did not choose the religious scholars, the Pharisees. He didn't choose the popular choices. He didn't choose the "reputable religious people" of society. He didn't choose the leaders validated by society. He simply chose the humble, "foolish" ones. In the Acts Church, some of the ones who carried the most spiritual wisdom were an ex-murderer (Paul), a fisherman (Peter) and a tax collector (Matthew). Will you be humble enough to hear the word of God when it comes through mentors/spiritual parents like that whom God chooses?

The society of Jesus' day would never have thought that such people carried true revelation from God. Yet Jesus uses the same type of people today, and often the reception they get is the same. We need to remember that it's the unlikely ones who are carrying the mysteries of the Kingdom. They come from all different countries, different skin colors, different ages, both male and female. It's common today to think God will speak through a person of a certain age or background, of a certain gender, and from a certain Bible school or from under a certain spiritual father/mother/mentor. But God is using the foolish things to confound the wisdom of this world: "Therefore once more I will astound these people with wonder upon wonder; the wisdom of the wise will perish, the intelligence of the intelligent will vanish" (Isaiah 29:14).

Today, many of the deeper revelations of the Kingdom come from modern-day "nobodies." The religious, pharisaic spirit has attacked me many times simply because of who my spiritual father is. He could be counted among those "foolish things" that confound this world's wisdom. His country in East Africa could be compared to Nazareth. And as a way to discount Jesus, people asked in His day, "What good comes from Nazareth?" I thank God for the grace He gave me to be childlike so I could receive teachings through my spiritual father about the Kingdom's secrets. We don't get to choose how we will hear God's voice. Many believers today are missing God's voice because they pridefully discount the vessel God is speaking to them through.

## GOD REPLACES WRONG THEOLOGY WITH TRUTH

Humility is also giving God permission to completely wreck your theology. The spirit of religion attacks the Body of Christ and influences Christians with its religious doctrine, which is the wrong revelation of the Word of God, not the true, life-giving revelation from the Holy Spirit. With that being said, there is a whole lot of wrong theology that God wants to take out and replace with His truth.

There is always more of God to be found. There is always more revelation to learn. We will never be at a place where we know everything there is to know about God and the spiritual realm. We will never be on the same level as God! Therefore, we better be humble when it comes to our spiritual knowledge. Whether you are on day one of being a Christian or day fifteen thousand, you should always have a teachable heart before God. You should always live in the truth that there is so much more for you to learn.

To be humble is to give God permission to take out whatever is not of Him—whatever mistaken theology, whatever you have erroneously been taught about Him and His Kingdom and everything you incorrectly believe He has told you. We should always leave room for error when it comes to our hearing from God. For example, I'm sure there has been at least one time when you thought, "God told me this!" But then you realized that it wasn't God who told you; it was your own desires, or perhaps the devil coming as an angel of light. And no wonder, for Satan himself masquerades as an angel of light (see 2 Corinthians 11:14).

You should tread lightly with saying "God told me," and you also should always be humble about receiving correction for what you think God told you. Many times, people want something so badly that they will tell themselves God told them, when God never told them. When you are humble, you will not be deceived by your own desires or by the "angel of light." For your whole life, you should come before God with a heart like this:

*Lord, I empty out everything I've been taught about you and everything I believe you've taught me, and I put it all before you. I give you permission to confound me and remove the wrong doctrine. It's okay if I was wrong. I humble myself. I give you permission to remove all that is not from you, and I give you permission to teach me brand-new things about you and your Kingdom that I've never heard of before, and that even contradicts what I believed was truth.*

This "emptying yourself before God" is a huge key to how I was able to receive the anointing. There was a lot of wrong religious doctrine inside me. I allowed God to take a lot out and completely confound me. As I saw all the ways I had been wrong in the past, it really humbled me. I am grateful to have gone through that process of being confounded, because now it keeps me humble. Instead of thinking I know everything, I remember I need God's grace every day to be in His will and a pure vessel for Him. Humility keeps me a teachable child before God, no matter how high He lifts me.

There is a huge difference between being a talented preacher knowledgeable about the Bible and being spiritual. There are many people who preach the Bible, but who are not spiritual.

To be spiritual is to understand the things of the spiritual realm, by the revelation of God. These revelations only come to those who are humble.

Before the apostle Peter was given the powerful anointing where just being under his shadow was enough for people in need, there came a test of his spiritual revelation. One day, Jesus asked His disciples who they thought He was:

> When Jesus came to the region of Caesarea Philippi, he asked his disciples, "Who do people say the Son of Man is?"
> They replied, "Some say John the Baptist; others say Elijah; and still others, Jeremiah or one of the prophets."
> "But what about you?" he asked. "Who do you say I am?"
> Simon Peter answered, "You are the Messiah, the Son of the living God."
>
> Matthew 16:13–16

Peter answered rightly that Jesus was the Messiah. Peter had humbled himself so much that he became truly spiritual. You can see Jesus' delight in Peter for humbling himself so much that God was able to reveal to him the realities of the spiritual realm. Directly after this test that Peter passed, Jesus told him, "I will give you the keys of the kingdom of heaven; whatever you bind on earth will be bound in heaven, and whatever you loose on earth will be loosed in heaven" (v. 19). God was therefore able to use Peter so mightily, building His Church on the foundation of Peter and the other apostles and prophets (see Ephesians 2:20).

## THE KEYS OF THE KINGDOM ARE VITAL

Jesus also gave Peter the keys of the Kingdom, as He said He would. The keys of the Kingdom are spiritual revelations about how to walk in the authority of Christ and in the anointing. The keys are spiritual revelations that unlock people from demonic chains, no matter how complex and heavy the chains are. The keys destroy the works of the devil and unlock the Kingdom of God here on earth. The keys unlock the healing, deliverance and abundant life Jesus has provided for all God's children.

The keys of the Kingdom are vital. You can't go inside a house without the keys. You can't access the secrets that unlock the fullness of God's Kingdom without the keys. Many Christians have not accessed the abundant life that Jesus paid a price for. Most are living in bondage because few in the Body of Christ actually have been given the keys to unlock other people's freedom and release the keys to others.

For the most part, deliverance today does not look the way it did in the early Church, the way the apostles Paul and Peter were casting out demons and the Bible says all who were tormented and sick were delivered and healed (see Acts 5:16). Many who cast out demons today are spending a long time trying to cast out one demon. Many today find in some cases the demons just don't leave, and they don't know why. Most who cast out demons today are not doing it with such little effort and such massive anointing, the way Peter and Paul did when just the touch of Paul's handkerchief or the shadow cast by Peter made the demons go.

These facts are meant to convict us as the Body of Christ. We should read the book of Acts and ask, *What are we missing?* Demons seemed to go so much more easily and quickly when Peter and Paul ministered. And at the early Church's services, *everyone* was healed! They must have had some revelation that much of today's Church does not have! As it says in Matthew 11:25–26, God reveals these spiritual things to the humble, and He hides them from the proud. This should speak to you and me, so that we think, *I need to humble myself more to receive more revelation and to fully receive the keys that were given to Peter and the Acts Church.*

A high level of humility like Peter had is required to receive the keys to the Kingdom. Out of all of those disciples who were close to Jesus, only Peter was humble enough in that moment we looked at in Matthew's gospel to spiritually perceive the truth and pass the test to access the keys of the Kingdom. We can't get lazy with humility. When you think you've gone low, go lower! The Bible says to *humble* yourself as an action word, something you should *do*. To access the keys, you can't stop short. You need to humble yourself continually, every day, and be prepared for tests of your humility.

# 5

# The Wilderness Process

... you have been grieved by various trials, so that the tested genuineness of your faith—more precious than gold that perishes though it is tested by fire—may be found to result in praise and glory and honor at the revelation of Jesus Christ.

1 Peter 1:6–7 ESV

Before you see the anointing flowing through you and miracles breaking out, there is an unavoidable step you must go through, and that step is the *process*. I also call this step the Wilderness Process. From Abraham to Joseph (son of Jacob), to the children of Israel, to David, to Jesus, there was always a wilderness season before entering the "promised land." The wilderness is uncomfortable, pushes your limits and is unavoidable. But it is an absolutely beautiful and necessary part of God's perfect plan for molding you into a vessel who can faithfully carry His precious anointing.

To carry the anointing, you must be seeking Christlike character. If God were to anoint someone whose character wasn't

Christlike, that person would abuse the anointing and become an agent of the devil, as well as misrepresenting Jesus to the world. This is a very serious deal. When you have the anointing, there is a spotlight on you. If a vessel misrepresents God and misuses the anointing, the kingdom of darkness does serious damage through that, which brings confusion and abuse to God's children.

Before John the Baptist and Jesus came, four hundred years had gone by without a prophet and without miracles. God waited until people would humble themselves, and then He released His anointing. When there are not vessels ready to carry the anointing, God waits until humility and repentance come. His anointing is so precious and valuable that He would never give it to someone who would not properly steward it. So the genuineness of your faith, which is more precious than gold, is first tested by various trials, as we just read in the passage from 1 Peter. That unavoidable testing becomes your wilderness.

The heart of Jesus comes by going through the process: "Behold, I have refined you, but not as silver; I have tried you in the furnace of affliction" (Isaiah 48:10 ESV). When gold is put through the fire, the impurities are removed and all that is left is pure gold. Oil comes when olives are pressed. Wine comes when grapes are crushed. What makes the anointing oil come into your life is the refining fire that takes away the impurities, and the pressing and crushing that molds your heart into the heart of Christ.

As soon as the word from God comes that you are called to be anointed and you say yes, you can expect the next step to be the wilderness process. Those who are called to be highly anointed go through a more intense wilderness and testing than those who have a different calling or those with a big calling who settle for less. We see all throughout the Bible that the bigger the calling, the bigger the testing. Also, the bigger the calling, the higher the level of the enemy's attacks. God will allow these attacks of the enemy because He uses the "pressure" that comes with them as a way to test you, and with every test passed, you allow God to put His hands on your heart and mold and refine your heart to be like His. In every case of the wilderness season, whatever the devil intended for harm, God will use for good.

The fruit of the Spirit includes "love, joy, peace, patience, kindness, goodness, faithfulness, gentleness, and self-control" (Galatians 5:22–23 NLT). Jesus is all of these things. God needs you to have these characteristics, too, before He can entrust you with the anointing. You don't need to have these characteristics completely perfected in you before God can first pour out anointing in your life, because it's a journey to be transformed into the image of Christ. But the Spirit's fruit should really be evident in your life as you continuously seek Jesus, before God entrusts you with the anointing.

The real you is a spirit. That is what came alive when you gave your life to Jesus, when you were born again and you became a new creation (see 2 Corinthians 5:17). But you also have a soul, which is your mind, will and emotions. Your soul then lives in a physical body. The way you become like Jesus is when your soul and flesh have been transformed so that they agree with and submit to your spirit, which is submitted to the Holy Spirit. Your spirit wants the things of God and wants to be like God immediately when you are born again. But when you are first born again, many times your soul and body are strong and need to be put in submission to the Holy Spirit so that they don't take over. When you first become a believer, and before your soul has been transformed, many times the desires of your mind, will and emotions won't naturally be the same as the Holy Spirit's desire.

For example, your spirit, one with the Holy Spirit and submitted to Him, wants to go to church. But your soul feels lazy and depressed, and feels like staying in bed. Your body, now following your soul's strong desires, just feels so tired!

Another example is when a person says something mean to you. Your spirit wants to respond with gentleness, kindness, patience and love. But your soul's desires are still more powerful than your spirit. Your soul is livid and offended. Your body follows your soul, and with a heart racing with anger, you burst out with mean words back at the person in a loud, aggressive voice.

When you give your life to Jesus, your soul needs to be transformed so that your spirit, soul and body reflect Jesus, and so that you think, feel, sound and look like Jesus. How does that happen? The way your soul and flesh are transformed is by seeking God:

> And we all, with unveiled face, continually seeing as in a mirror the glory of the Lord, are progressively being transformed into His image from [one degree of] glory to [even more] glory, which comes from the Lord, [who is] the Spirit.
>
> 2 Corinthians 3:18 AMP

When I surrendered to God, my biggest desire became to please Him and be in His will. A passion erupted in me to see Him be pleased with me, to hear Him say "well done, good and faithful servant" every day. That became all I wanted. And then when God called me to be an apostle, a great reverence for God came over me. I could feel the seriousness of what He had called me to. He didn't have to choose me. Who was I, for Him to choose me for such a big calling? He was entrusting me with so much! He was counting on me to represent Him well. So now, obeying Jesus was not only my biggest passion, but was also my greatest responsibility.

This is step one to receiving God's heart: *Decide that your mission on this earth is to obey God every single day.* This is the action of giving God permission to have His way completely in your life. This is the action of giving God permission to do spiritual surgery on your heart. Without this intention, your soul will automatically be the leader and win every time. This is what happens when you follow your feelings. Without putting Jesus first, you follow the world's way and human instinct's way. Whatever you feel, you speak. Whatever you want to do, you do.

When you live that way, your spirit is dormant and is over-powered by your soul. You can call yourself a Christian, but you are not being transformed into the image of God, and you don't look or sound like Jesus. This is not a good representation of Him to the world, and it doesn't shine His light to the world. It doesn't attract the lost and is actually a bad witness. Soulish Christians tend to push people away from God because they say they are Christian, but they instead look just like the world.

When you make it your intention for your spirit to follow the Holy Spirit, this is the action of seeking God. You are looking to Him to help lead you and empower you to think, speak and act in a way that always pleases Him. When you do this, you are taking the action of making your spirit lead instead of your soul. Your spirit becomes the leader, and it does whatever the Holy Spirit says. Then the soul and flesh must follow, so your entire being is looking, sounding and acting like Christ.

## A JUDGING HEART OR A LOVING HEART?

You can know the Holy Spirit's voice by reading the Word of God and meditating on it. One of the biggest areas where our hearts need to be transformed is in loving those we may feel like judging. For example, when you feel the urge to judge a person, this Scripture will give you guidance on how you should actually act:

> Why do you look at the speck of sawdust in your brother's eye and pay no attention to the plank in your own eye? How can

you say to your brother, "Let me take the speck out of your eye," when all the time there is a plank in your own eye? You hypocrite, first take the plank out of your own eye, and then you will see clearly to remove the speck from your brother's eye.

Matthew 7:3–5

So now, before blasting someone on the Internet, "canceling" the person, gossiping behind his or her back and stewing hatred in your heart, you can renew your mind with the Word of God. Instead of letting your soul take over, you can remember how God sees the person and how He wants you to see and treat him or her. You can instead choose to bless and pray for that person, holding your tongue when it's tempting to gossip and speak bad, judgmental things. You can repent for the hatred you felt in your heart and ask God to help you see the person as He does.

Humble yourself. When you are judging someone, automatically you have a bigger flaw than the person you're judging. That's how serious and wrong judging someone else is. That person just has a "speck," but you have a "plank." Now you should spend time dealing with your plank by taking it to God and humbling yourself. You should acknowledge that there is judgment, righteousness and pride in your heart and that you really don't want them there. Tell God and surrender it all to Him. Your tendency to judge has made you aware that this part of your soul is stronger than the humility part of your spirit. This means you need to be extra intentional to see people with love. Always renew your mind as you view people, remembering that God loves them so much and wants them so blessed.

Many Christians look at someone they disprove of and desire that the person fail and be shamed. Before God can entrust you with the anointing, He needs you to have a heart like His, a heart that loves people no matter their past and no matter what they are currently doing. We need to view every single person with these eyes of grace and mercy. We need to desire to see people transformed and highly blessed! That is a rare heart, but it's possible when you allow God to do daily spiritual surgery on your heart.

As you make it your intention every day to do what Jesus would do in every situation, it makes your spirit become stronger and your soul and flesh weaker (the carnal tendencies). You will find at first it can be hard to love people who are difficult to love. But over time, as you do the spiritual work to deny your flesh and intentionally love others, you will find it gets easier and becomes more natural. Eventually, hate and judgment are not even part of you anymore. You naturally see others with love and grace. Your heart has been transformed to be like God's!

## THE WILDERNESS SEASON

To have a heart like Jesus, you have to intentionally do your part in denying your flesh and becoming more spiritual. In the process, there is a place God will lead you to make your heart as much like His as possible. He brings the fire to take out all the impurities. Before the refining fire, you may have the fruit of the Spirit, but the "wilderness" we talked about at the beginning of this chapter is where perfecting happens. There is more!

The Bible says, "Be perfect, therefore, as your heavenly Father is perfect" (Matthew 5:48). God wants you to come out shiny and like gold—not just "good enough," but dazzling so much that people are amazed at the Jesus you reflect and the Jesus they encounter through you. Paul did *extraordinary* miracles. Don't you want to be *extraordinarily* like God? That's what God wants for you, because then He can use you even more powerfully.

I had been denying my flesh and submitting my soul and flesh to my spirit, following the Holy Spirit, for a year before receiving my calling, and I had seen such radical transformation. But looking back, I see that God was just getting started. At that point, it was not yet time for me to enter the wilderness, but that season was coming for me.

Jesus had been following His Father since boyhood, studying the Word of God in the Temple and synagogue, and obeying the Father all His life. But when Jesus was thirty and it was about time for Him to begin His ministry and do what He was created for, then the Holy Spirit led Him into the wilderness. Here there were tests, and with the passing of the tests came the refining. It was the perfecting process before Jesus walked in His calling and demonstrated the love of the Father to the world.

When you have a big calling to be anointed, there is a more intensive refining process in the wilderness. It's where you go from facing normal trials in life to facing extreme testing. It certainly isn't easy, nor comfortable. Everyone's wilderness season will look different. The length of your wilderness season depends on your specific calling, and also on your obedience. Will you wander around like the Israelites in the desert, or will you take the direct way?

There will also be different seasons of wilderness in life before you reach the next level of anointing. Before I saw the fulfillment of my promise from God—that He would do many miracles through me, that I would reach the nations, and that revival would break out in my ministry and spread across the United States and then the world—I went through a wilderness season of four and a half years. And those years were *deep* in the wilderness, deeper and drier than I had ever imagined.

Joseph's wilderness process was long and deep, too. God gave him a dream that made his brothers jealous:

> Joseph had a dream, and when he told it to his brothers, they hated him all the more. He said to them, "Listen to this dream I had: We were binding sheaves of grain out in the field when

suddenly my sheaf rose and stood upright, while your sheaves gathered around mine and bowed down to it."

His brothers said to him, "Do you intend to reign over us? Will you actually rule us?" And they hated him all the more because of his dream and what he had said.

Genesis 37:5–8

His brothers' jealousy became so bad that it became hate. This led them to throw him into a pit to die. Shortly after, they decided to sell him as a slave instead to some Ishmaelites on their way to Egypt. So Joseph was given this amazing dream from God, and shortly after, he entered a wilderness season where God refined him as he passed through trials and tests. Joseph became a slave in Egypt. One day, the wife of his master made up a lie about him when he refused to come to bed with her. The master believed the lie and threw Joseph in jail (see Genesis 39). From being in the pit, to being a slave, to being in prison, Joseph was being refined as he passed each test. He passed these tests of faith and obedience as he kept his faith alive in the darkest moments, as he never forsook God, and as he continued to be obedient to Him. He kept praising God through it all, and even in prison he was a blessing to the other prisoners.

David was another example of someone in an extreme wilderness season. The Bible says of him, "For the Lord has sought out a man after his own heart" (1 Samuel 13:14 NLT). David had a beautiful, godly heart and was a faithful servant of God. Then he was anointed to be king. Even though he was godly and had this amazing heart, there was still more refining to be done. There were several years between the time David was anointed by the prophet Samuel and the time he actually became king. He was taken through the wilderness, facing attack after attack from King Saul.

The favor of God was upon David mightily, so much so that he was very successful in defeating his enemies. Yet his victories brought even more attacks toward him. One time when the troops returned home from yet another victory, look what happened when the women of Israel came out to greet them:

> As they danced, they sang: "Saul has slain his thousands, and David his tens of thousands."
>
> Saul was very angry; this refrain displeased him greatly. "They have credited David with tens of thousands," he thought, "but me with only thousands. What more can he get but the kingdom?" And from that time on Saul kept a close eye on David.
>
> The next day an evil spirit from God came forcefully on Saul. He was prophesying in his house, while David was playing the lyre, as he usually did. Saul had a spear in his hand and he hurled it, saying to himself, "I'll pin David to the wall." But David eluded him twice.
>
> 1 Samuel 18:7–11

Once jealousy entered the heart of King Saul, David faced the greatest challenges of his life. From that point on, Saul tried to kill David again and again and again. At one point, Saul sent his armies to kill David and David had to run for his life and hide. This season was David's wilderness. God used this season to refine David so that his heart that was after God's heart could be perfected through the pressure.

David still praised God through such difficult moments. All over the psalms he wrote, you can see his victory through the trials. It was David who said, "Even though I walk through the darkest valley, I will fear no evil, for you are with me; your rod and your staff, they comfort me" (Psalm 23:4). Even in the darkest valleys, David was speaking to his soul and making it submit to the Spirit's will, which was for him to praise God and keep hope alive: "Why, my soul, are you downcast? Why so disturbed within me? Put your hope in God, for I will yet praise him, my Savior and my God" (Psalm 43:5).

Joseph didn't imagine that when he announced his dream, his brothers would be so full of jealousy that they would throw him into a pit and sell him as a slave. David didn't imagine that after being anointed as king and becoming a successful warrior, he would be hunted by King Saul and his army purely out of jealousy. If God revealed to us what our wilderness would look like, too many of us would give up before we even began. But God will not give you anything you cannot handle! "The temptations in your life are no different from what others experience. And God is faithful. He will not allow the temptation to be more than you can stand. When you are tempted, he will show you a way out so that you can endure" (1 Corinthians 10:13 NLT).

## MY WILDERNESS

When I obeyed God and stepped into my calling of being an apostle and the leader of a church, I stepped into the most uncomfortable season of my life. In life, we tend to gravitate toward the things we are good at and where we feel comfortable. We tend to avoid the uncomfortable. Singing was comfortable and easy for me. Preaching was my biggest fear. Public speaking was literally the only thing that would make me nervous.

For most of my life, I have been fearless. I have been skydiving twice, both times supernaturally feeling absolutely no fear. I have cliff jumped from very high cliffs. I traveled the world on a cruise ship for four months with hundreds of students, none of whom I knew prior. I moved out to Los Angeles by myself, where I had no friends or family, just a couple of acquaintances. And I drove out to LA from New York by myself. I was the lead in my high school musical for three years, and I had no fear of singing and acting in front of hundreds of people. I have had this natural courage in me since I was a kid. But the one thing that scared me was speaking off-the-cuff in front of people, unscripted. In middle school I was afraid to talk to people I didn't know or wasn't close to. I only talked to my close friends, and I felt so insecure about my social skills. The moment I saw people looking at me as I said something, I would freeze.

By God's grace, I finally came out of my shell and was transformed into an outgoing person by high school. Yet public speaking was still something I was afraid of. In college, I would sometimes have to do group presentations in front of a class. Even in front of only ten people, I would freeze and get knots in my stomach. Whenever I had to do a presentation, I felt as if I would go brain-dead, and I wouldn't know what to say. Even after college, when I would be in a Bible study and would say something in front of ten people (just like a "hello, this is a fact about me"), I would get so nervous! Leading a group of people was also my weakness. Throughout college, I would never volunteer to lead group projects, even if there were only three people in the group. I always sat back and waited for someone else to lead. I felt as if I didn't know how to be a leader.

And now, God was calling *me* to be a preacher whose job it was to speak in front of people constantly and to lead a church?! These were literally my biggest weaknesses. These things made me the most uncomfortable. On top of that, I had no clue how I could be a preacher who got revelation from God and preached sermons at least once a week! I had only spoken a "sermon" one time, and it was more like sharing my testimony in front of students in college. So now I had received this prophecy, and God was calling me to begin preaching every week and to start a church in nine months. Talk about uncomfortable and scary! I wasn't really scared, though. Even in my discomfort, I always trusted God. I trusted that He somehow would make me into a preacher and give me words to speak. I just couldn't picture it and couldn't imagine how it was going to happen.

Our first 5F Church service was June 18, 2017. We first held services outside, on a mountaintop on Mulholland Drive, overlooking the Valley in Los Angeles. The first time I preached,

there were two other people there (friends who were supporting me), and no one else showed up. Even though it was just
preaching to my friends, I felt so nervous and uncertain. But
God gave me words to speak. I started posting about our services
on Facebook groups, and between one and ten people would
come, depending on the week. Week after week, I would stand
up there and strum my guitar that I had taught myself to play.
I wasn't very good, but there was no one else and it got the job
done. I would lead worship, and then I would preach.

Every week that I preached, I would hear the enemy speaking lies:

—*You're not a good enough preacher for people to want
to listen to you. You're not blessing people.*
—*The other preachers in the world are so much better
than you.*
—*These people are bored. Look at their faces; they're not
interested. They probably won't be back.*

It wasn't easy pushing past those lies and preaching anyway.
God taught me what true confidence is as I preached week
after week. True confidence is not being void of the feelings of
fear. True confidence is when, even though you are hearing the
enemy's lies trying to feed your fear, you push past them and
do what God has called you to do, despite your feelings.

So I didn't *feel* confident, literally for years. But I *was* confident from day one, because I was saying no to the devil's lies. I
kept preaching with firmness and boldness, despite what I was
feeling inside. I really had to rely on God completely when it
came to preaching. Every week, I would feel as though I had
nothing else to preach. I even felt like that after the very first
week. And then it continued for years. I would dread every
Saturday because it meant my time was running short to figure

out what I would preach on Sunday, and to prepare the sermon. Of course, God gave me the words. And let me tell you, He came through every time!

Sometimes, I would be afraid that I would show up to church and literally have no clue what to say. It was such an uncomfortable feeling. But this made it so that I had to rely on God rather than on my own strength. I am so grateful for this. Before preaching, I would always say, *God, I need you. There's no way I can do this without you. I need you to give me words, because I have none on my own!*

I would be amazed every week as God came through and gave me words to preach. Jeanntal would always tell me after every service that the word I preached had blessed her so much and was powerful. Oh, how that blessed me! I *needed* that encouragement of the Lord through her because the voices of the enemy were loud, and usually no one else would share with me that they were blessed by the word. God used Jeanntal to build me up and give me confidence in my preaching, and I can't imagine where I would be without her constant encouraging words.

## NOT OUT OF THE WILDERNESS YET

When I said yes to God's calling on my life, I was saying yes purely out of obedience, not because I desired it. For some reason I thought, *Well, maybe since I don't want to do this, at least God won't make it so difficult for it to happen.* But seeing revival break out like what had been prophesied looked farther and farther away every year that passed. The first year, there were about twenty people in the church at one point. By the second year, there were about fifteen. The third year, there were ten. By 2020, there were five. When we took church outside in 2020 after Covid hit, sometimes it was truly just Jeanntal and me.

I didn't know how God was going to accomplish His plan, but I had guessed that we would gradually grow little by little each year. At least ten more people each year? Instead, the church got smaller and smaller. To be truthful, this was really discouraging. Especially because one of the enemy's nasty schemes was usually the reason that people left, "for he is a liar and the father of lies" (John 8:44). The enemy would speak lies about the ministry. It was heartbreaking to see church family, people whom you loved deeply, believe a lie of the enemy and suddenly leave.

It also kept feeling as if our tiny church couldn't measure up to the many megachurch choices in Los Angeles. I cried out to God, *Lead people to our church who just want you! Who just want your presence and nothing else! Who value your precious anointing!* I prayed, *Lord, I don't want people to come to 5F Church because of an entertaining/comedic/intellectual/fancy-sounding sermon, a good-sounding worship band, flashy lights, a fancy building, or to socialize, flirt, show off their outfit, or come for the "church activities." I want people to come for only one reason—to encounter you! To have a true encounter with your power and to be in your presence! I don't want them to leave thinking, "What a talented speaker." Instead, I want them thinking, "Jesus, Jesus, Jesus, what you did—wow! You are amazing, Jesus!" I want people to leave 5F Church services feeling so in awe of you, Lord, that nothing else can take your place in their minds.*

I started to wonder where those people were, and if they would ever find us. Usually, only about one new person would come to church each month. God would usually touch that person powerfully through prophetic ministry, but then he or she usually would not come back. *Maybe all the empty chairs were a turnoff,* I would think. We moved forward with two services every week. Sometimes, zero other people would show up to worship night, except for three of us. I would be there in person, and Jeanntal and Fred (who played bass) would come. That was it. Sometimes, just the three of us would spend hours setting up all the equipment for a service no one would show up to (or just one or two other people)! And I would tell Jeanntal and Fred, "Let's worship with all our hearts, because years from now people will go on Facebook and watch these old livestreams and will have encounters with God through our worship. He is worthy to be praised alone, even if it is just the three of us." (And indeed, people have testified of watching the old livestreams and being touched by God as they watched.)

At times, I held back tears as I led worship, looking at the empty chairs. But I stayed strong and kept declaring the faithfulness and goodness of God. I would declare *Revival Is Now* when there was just one person in the congregation. I believed in that prophetic word with all my heart, and I knew that God was calling me to keep declaring it until we saw it come to pass. So I just kept going. Because the church was getting smaller each year, it felt as though we were going backward rather than forward. I would feel that way, and then God would remind me of Joseph's wilderness. After Joseph received his dream, was thrown into a pit to die and then was thrown in prison, I'm sure he felt as if he were going farther away from his dream instead of closer. But really, in the spiritual realm he was getting closer and closer with each trial he overcame and with each test he passed.

The most difficult part of my wilderness was the persecution I faced. Before I stepped into my calling and began walking in the anointing, I really didn't face too much spiritual warfare, and I don't believe I was ever really persecuted. But as soon as I stepped into my calling, wow! The level of persecution shocked me. Some people became jealous of me and did awful things to me behind my back. They made up some terrible lies about me and the ministry. About fifteen people left the church in the first year as a result, when there were only twenty to begin with!

Then someone called the place where we rented our building and made up another disgusting lie to try to get the owner to stop renting to us. The owner could tell it was a lie and continued renting to us anyway. Somehow, the people spreading these lies found my parents' address, and they told my parents lies, hoping my parents would stop supporting me. But my parents knew the truth and have never stopped supporting me to this day.

I couldn't believe this kind of spiritual warfare was coming against us in just the first year. This actually encouraged me as I set my eyes on the truth in the spiritual realm. The only thing that made sense was that the devil was terrified of the anointing and calling upon my life, and he wanted to stop me in my tracks before I became too dangerous to his kingdom.

Through all these hard times, I kept my joy and peace because I kept my eyes on Jesus. My sole desire was to please God and be in His will. I wanted nothing else. Thanks to the Word of God, and to reading the stories of Joseph and David, I understood that this wilderness period I was going through was necessary. I had to go against my Goliath, but Jesus would help me be victorious. I would have a "Saul" chasing me down and trying to kill my ministry and me, but with Jesus I would be victorious. Nothing would stop God's plan for my life; I would only come out stronger.

I understood that I just had to go through the refining fire. I remember one time speaking to my soul through tears, as David had spoken to his soul: *Why are you downcast, O my soul?*

I felt weary from all the attacks, but I reminded myself of this truth: *I don't even deserve to carry God's precious anointing and walk in the high-level calling He has assigned to me. Even fifty years would not be enough time in the refining fire and in the wilderness for me to "deserve" or be worthy of this calling.*

I humbled myself. I told myself, *I better not complain about this wilderness, because this is the necessary molding of my heart that must take place to reach God's will for my life. If I complain, I'm fighting God and being like the Israelites in the wilderness, who just delayed their destiny because they were fighting the necessary and beautiful process ordained by God.*

Through tears I would say, *Thank you, God, for taking me through the fire. I thank you that you're in control and that you know exactly how to refine me. You know exactly what I must go through, and your plan and timing are perfect. Thank you that I'm in your hands. Thank you for this beautiful calling and precious anointing that you have entrusted to me.*

God strengthened me, and I never got depressed or felt like giving up. Giving up was never a thought because that would mean I would be out of God's will and I would grieve Him. There is nothing worse in the world than that. I kept my eyes on Jesus and remained in perfect peace: "You will keep in perfect peace all who trust in you, all whose thoughts are fixed on you!" (Isaiah 26:3 NLT). Oh, how true that Scripture is. Jesus can really give you peace and comfort and even supernatural joy in the most difficult circumstances.

## A GREAT TRANSFORMATION

By year four of the wilderness, I noticed a great transformation that had taken place. The first couple of years were very difficult since each week I was doing something I didn't enjoy all that much. I was just purely obeying God. At the same time, because it was a difficult period, I found myself absolutely longing for dreams that I had always had in life. It had always been my dream to have a family, to have a husband and children. But when I was facing this most difficult time of my life, I suddenly fiercely longed for these dreams. Looking back, I see that it was as if I wanted at least one dream to be fulfilled to get me through this difficult season.

God taught me through this, however, that we want some dreams so badly because we think their coming to pass will fill a void and bring some comfort and happiness we are missing.

But Jesus is the only one who can fill the void in us with contentment. He is the only one who brings true joy and peace. Dreams fulfilled are blessings, icing on the cake, that bring more beauty to life. But really, Jesus is enough! Jesus alone really can fill every single void in your life.

I am so glad God didn't give me what I wanted when I wanted it, because then I wouldn't know that He truly can fill my every void. This is part of the refining fire. God needs to replace with Himself voids in your life that you have filled with other things, or haven't allowed Him to fill yet, as you have held the space for a future dream. To use you the most powerfully, He needs every single part of you.

Through tears at times, longing for my dreams, I would say, *Let your will be done, God. I give you all my dreams, even my dream of having a family. I surrender it to you! And if it is your will that I have a family, I only want it in Your timing.* Oh, I wanted my dream so badly right then and there! But I only spoke, *Let your will be done. Only give me my dreams when it's your timing.* God convicted me to be so sensitive about never allowing the devil to get a foothold by letting my will get in the way of God's will.

By the fourth year of the wilderness, I noticed that I was transformed. My desires were transformed. I no longer painfully longed for those dreams; I was just content for God to give me only His dreams, and whenever He wanted to. Every year until that fourth year of the wilderness, I had desperately longed for "this to be the year that the promise would come to pass" (the promise of revival). But by the fourth year, I suddenly felt so content. Covid even hit, which made it feel as if we went backward even further. We went from five to seven people in our church services to being only online for a couple of months, where it was just me showing up in person, along with Jeanntal and her parents. Then we began having church outside, where there would sometimes just be two of us. Through all of that,

I felt supernatural contentment. God had refined me so much that my soul was now matching my spirit. I thought, *Whatever, God. Wherever, God. I know you are in control. I know your timing is perfect. I trust you.* Year four, I could finally relate to the apostle Paul when he said,

> I am not saying this because I am in need, for I have learned to be content whatever the circumstances. I know what it is to be in need, and I know what it is to have plenty. I have learned the secret of being content in any and every situation, whether well fed or hungry, whether living in plenty or in want.
>
> Philippians 4:11–12

All I want is to be in God's will. So whatever God's will is, I am content there. In the hard times, I'm there because God needs me to be there to refine me, so I can be more like Him and He can elevate me for His glory and for His work to be done. So there's no place I'd rather be. In the good times, I am content there also, not because they are happy times that make me feel good, but simply because I'm in God's will. Sometimes God's will is just not fun. But whether fun or difficult, there's no place I'd rather be!

When Covid hit, God told me to go live online and preach every single day from March 2020 until October 2020. I had grown in my preaching a lot by then. It wasn't as uncomfortable as at first, and I would truly feel joy to preach. God had refined my heart so I had revelation that my words were encouraging and blessing others. That gave me joy and the excitement to minister.

The voice of the enemy was still there, though, pointing out how the church had gotten smaller, and also pointing out that when I was going live online every day, sometimes zero people were watching. I would literally see the number on Instagram go from one person viewing to none. During the lockdowns, every day I would go for a walk, enjoy nature and be with God, and then go live. I didn't fear Covid, because God had refined me never to fear. I knew that Covid and the resulting lockdowns were not stopping or delaying God's promises. I learned to be content and have great joy during the time when everything was shut down. I could see that I truly had been transformed.

The year that I felt so content in the "waiting" for the first time was the same year that God released the fulfillment of the promise! I had been transformed hugely, and as I look back, I can see that I was now ready to receive the promise. It was December 30, 2020, when I posted the video that went viral. On the last day of 2020 (most people's "worst year"), that video going viral was to me like the walls of Jericho coming down. Everything changed from that day, from that one video!

## WORKING RELENTLESSLY AND WITH JOY

Looking back, I can see God's beautiful and intentional refining fire upon my heart. With each trial I overcame, I can look back and say that I was truly transformed more into His image after going through it. All you have to do is obey, and once you obey, God does the molding. Just obey, and God then transforms you. By showing up to preach when I didn't want to, over and over and over, God transformed me into a preacher—a confident preacher who has a lot to teach now! I used to be afraid I wouldn't teach long enough, but now I have to make sure I don't preach too long because God gives me so much to teach and so much passion about building and encouraging others. I see how God has transformed me so much and has opened my spiritual eyes, and I want that so badly for other people now. I want them blessed as much as God has blessed me. I want them to have victory over the enemy and be powerful anointed vessels of God.

When I first received the call, I had no desire to both preach and pray for people. I wanted people to encounter the power of God and know His love more than anything, but I was happy being on the sidelines and not actually being the one praying for people or preaching. But now, it's my absolute biggest passion to pray for others and teach God's Word. To be a vessel of God and see someone set free and encounter the love of Jesus right before my eyes is my very biggest passion in the world.

The passion to minister now far surpasses my original greatest passion of singing. My sole passion is to be in God's will and do what He has called me to do—minister. Even with my dream of having a family, for the first time I feel so content that it can truly be *whenever*. It can be many years from now, and I truly feel content with that. *Whatever is God's will!* As I write this, I can't even believe I'm saying that. That's how much of a supernatural work God has done in me. God has given me His passions. He has given me His heart for His people, which causes me to work for Him relentlessly and with joy.

Through this wilderness, God has refined my heart to be patient. I was once so anxious for the promised land to come. Yet through day after day, year after year of choosing not to complain and choosing to keep obeying God, that heart of patience was formed in me. In moments when I am yearning for something to come, I now say, *Not my will, but your will, God. I want your will, which includes your timing. So if it's not your timing yet, I am content to keep waiting.*

It's not always easy, but when you are brought through the refining fire, you become a person of patience. You no longer complain or get into a rut when the "wait time" is long; instead, you choose only to praise God and stay focused on pleasing Him. I have learned through the process to enjoy every single day and thank God for the many blessings He gives me. There is too much to be grateful for to be impatient.

## TRUSTING GOD, LOVING OUR ENEMIES

Through the wilderness, God also taught me how to love my enemies like never before. I told you a little already about how I had never faced such situations full of jealousy, hate, backstabbing and being cursed at before in my life. But I faced them in the wilderness! This really molded my heart to be able to love even in the most difficult circumstances.

The love came in this training of denying myself and never saying what another person "deserved," or speaking against him or her. I learned to always be gentle, kind, slow to speak and full of love. In moments when people were spreading lies about the ministry and me, I had to trust in God like never before. I had to trust that He would truly defend me. I had to trust that if people believed the lies and left the church, it would be okay. I had to trust that God would fulfill His promise, no matter how impossible it seemed. As I trusted Him in these hard circumstances, my trust in Him grew more and more. Malicious actions toward me bothered me less and less. God was preparing me for bigger trials and attacks ahead.

I also told you earlier that as the anointing increases, so does the persecution. The more of a threat you are to the devil's kingdom, the harder he tries to stop you. Since 2021 when the first demon was cast out, millions of people now follow my ministry on social media and watch 5F Church and my "Revival Is Now" events around the world on YouTube. I have been ministering at revival events every week in different states and in ten different countries (so far), as well as ministering every Sunday at 5F Church in Los Angeles. As my platform grew and I became more well-known, I started facing higher-level spiritual attacks and persecution than I ever had before. Videos full of false accusations were made to "expose me," bringing up my past, twisting my words and taking things out of context. I have even had the most vicious accusation of all spoken about me, which the Pharisees first said about Jesus: "It is only by Beelzebul, the prince of demons, that this fellow drives out demons" (Matthew 12:24).

This hasn't been easy, and there have been some heartbreaking moments of seeing people be deceived by such lies. In those moments, the only thing I could do was to lean on Jesus and His Word like never before. Matthew 5:10–12 provides so much strength:

> Blessed are those who are persecuted because of righteousness, for theirs is the kingdom of heaven.
>
> Blessed are you when people insult you, persecute you and falsely say all kinds of evil against you because of me. Rejoice and be glad, because great is your reward in heaven, for in the same way they persecuted the prophets who were before you.

When you become like Jesus in the fruits, the gifts of the Spirit and the anointing, you begin to face the same attacks and accusations that Jesus did, because it is Jesus who is inside you. It is Satan attacking Jesus inside you. It was Satan through the Pharisees attacking Jesus, and now it is Satan through the "Pharisees" of today attacking Jesus inside us. Instead of allowing these attacks to scare, intimidate or offend me, I chose to believe this spiritual reality: *These attacks are inevitable for God to lift us to the next level, and for more souls to be reached.*

Persecution is inevitable. As Jesus said, you are blessed when you are persecuted. It's a blessing to be persecuted for righteousness' sake. It's a blessing to be that big of a threat to the devil, that he brings his most extreme attacks against you. It's a blessing to be able to surrender and sacrifice for Jesus at a deeper level. It's a blessing to please God in this new way through your obedience to Him.

## GOD IS OUR DEFENDER

Remember that God is your defender. Nothing can stop the move of God. People can scheme and plot against you, but they can never stop God's plan for your life. As the prophet Elisha told his servant, "Do not be afraid, for those who are with us are more than those who are with them" (2 Kings 6:16 AMP). You may face many enemies and people who have been deceived by the enemy, but there are people out there with pure, humble hearts, who have eyes to see. There are real disciples out there like Jesus' disciples, who had pure hearts to see who Jesus was and not believe the lies the top religious leaders of the time were spreading about Him. You don't need people's validation, only God's. It is not people who open doors for you, but God alone. If God could protect and preserve David's life and calling when Saul sent his army to kill him, then surely God will protect you.

Through all the difficulties I saw God bring me through in the wilderness, I always *knew* He would be faithful again. I knew it because of the uncountable times He has been faithful to me in the past. Not once has He let me down. I knew I could trust Him fully, so much that I could rest and have peace in the valley of the shadow of death (see Psalm 23:4). I knew He would bring me through persecution and I would come out yet again more refined and able to shine more brightly for Him, for His glory.

I can see how all those trials God took me through in the wilderness prepared me for my greatest test yet of public persecution, slander and character assassination. If I hadn't gone through all those trials in the wilderness, I don't think I would have made it through this difficult test. God gave me the strength to keep ministering in my rigorous travel schedule, without skipping a beat. He also gave me strength not to lash out at my enemies, but instead to stay quiet and rest under the shadow of His wings, where He was protecting me and fighting for me.

God gave me the ability to love and forgive those who persecuted me. The nasty weapons formed against me did not prosper. The work of God continued. I continued to travel weekly to different states and countries in the midst of the most intense persecution. God continued to bring hundreds and thousands to every event, delivering and healing His people. The anointing increased. The miracles increased. Every single week, hundreds continued to pour into the park for 5F Church's "Revival in the Park." Weekly, many people kept traveling from out of state and even from different countries to visit 5F Church, with God doing astounding miracles every time.

## "MINI-WILDERNESS" EXPERIENCES

There is usually one major wilderness preparation season before God begins to release you in your calling and you see the anointing flowing out of you. Then after that, there will certainly be more trials up ahead that can sometimes be like "mini-wildernesses." Remember that each battle prepares you for the next higher-level one.

Also remember, however, that with every single battle there is a reward. There is an increase of the anointing. In Christ, we go from glory to glory: "But we all, with unveiled face, beholding as in a mirror the glory of the Lord, are being transformed into the same image from glory to glory, just as by the Spirit of the Lord" (2 Corinthians 3:18 NKJV).

As you obey God day by day, God wants to increase your anointing so He can use you more and more, so more people can be reached with His love in this world. Yes, with every new level there will be a battle. And the reward of winning that battle will be a new level of anointing. With this spiritual perspective, it makes the battles not so bad to face. It can even make them exciting! You are a guaranteed champion, so it is exciting to enter into battle. There is victory and reward on the other side.

God is the one fighting for you, so you can't lose. All you have to do is be still and know that He is God (see Psalm 46:10). Renewing your mind with this spiritual reality is the way that you will maintain your peace and work for Him relentlessly, with joy.

# 6

# The Power of Impartation

In the last days, God says, I will pour out my Spirit on all people. Your sons and daughters will prophesy, your young men will see visions, your old men will dream dreams.

Acts 2:17

So far, you have learned how to be a vessel whom God can entrust with the anointing. Now you will learn the ways in which this anointing comes to fill you. God releases anointing to a vessel in two different ways. The first one is the less common way, and that is directly from Him, without a human vessel releasing the anointing. Elijah and Moses are examples of this. In the Bible, we don't hear about anointing being released from another vessel to them. God spoke to Moses through a burning bush, and the anointing began to work in his life after that encounter. God usually releases anointing in this way when He wants to start a new move and there are few people (or none) who carry the specific anointing He wants to release.

The second and most common way to receive the anointing is through impartation from another person. To *impart* means to bestow, transmit or pass on. When it comes to moving in miraculous power, God has chosen to move through human vessels. He could release miracles straight from heaven, without using a vessel, and there are exceptions where He does that. There are times when people receive miracles without God moving through a human vessel to bring one about. But for the most part, God chooses to move through vessels.

God chose to speak through vessels to write the entire Bible. The Bible contains God's words fully, but it didn't just appear out of thin air. People like you and me wrote the whole Bible! Sometimes I think we tend to forget that. It is 100 percent God's Word, but God's Word came through His vessels.

The number of Christians who experience healing and deliverance today without a vessel releasing the anointing would be a small percentage. Compare it to the number of people who received miracles through vessels of God in the Acts Church. The Acts Church is our example of how we should be disciples of Christ and how the Church should operate today. Many read Acts as just a history book, but it is truly our blueprint. We should do exactly as the Acts Church did. When it comes to the structure and operation of the Church, we should follow their example to a T. The Bible shows us how people were healed and delivered in the Acts Church:

> People brought the sick into the streets and laid them on beds and mats so that at least Peter's shadow might fall on some of them as he passed by. Crowds gathered also from the towns around Jerusalem, bringing their sick and those tormented by impure spirits, and all of them were healed.
>
> Acts 5:15–16

Peter was an apostle. His ministry took place mostly in a church setting, a gathering of believers to worship, hear a word and encounter Jesus. So when people were sick and demon possessed, the answer for their healing was very simple. They were brought to where the anointing was flowing through true appointed and anointed vessels of God (like Peter), vessels who carried high-level anointing to deal even with demonic principalities. This is why it says they were *all* healed. All were healed because the people were getting in line with God's way of releasing His power. Vessels like Peter and Paul were operating in high-level anointing and authority where even the highest-level demons had to obey.

This is God's way of releasing His power. Yes, He can move in other ways, without a vessel. But those are exceptions. God can move however He wants, of course, because of His great love for His people. But His main way of releasing miraculous power is through vessels. So when we get into alignment with how He moves, that's when we come under the waterfall of His anointing, as opposed to being at a distance and receiving only the mist from the waterfall. Under the waterfall is where we can see great miracles with ease! It's not supposed to be something difficult and rare to find His miracles. We simply need to do things God's way, and then we will be immersed in His miraculous power.

In the same way that God uses vessels most of the time to speak to His people and to do miracles, God also uses vessels to release the anointing to other vessels through impartation so they may walk in the power of God as well. This is God's main system of releasing anointing to His people. All throughout the Word of God, from the Old Testament to the New Testament, God releases His anointing from one vessel to another. Elisha received anointing from Elijah. Joshua received anointing from Moses. Timothy received anointing from Paul.

The Body of Christ in the Acts Church received impartation from elders (leaders): "Do not neglect the spiritual gift you received through the prophecy spoken over you when the elders of the church laid their hands on you" (1 Timothy 4:14

NLT). *Elders* means leaders in the Church who were anointed and were experienced in walking in the anointing. We can see through this passage that since they were releasing spiritual gifts, they themselves had a higher-level anointing to be able to release this impartation to others.

In every one of these situations of anointing being released in the Bible, the ones releasing it are not random ministers a receiving vessel comes across. Rather, they are God-appointed spiritual fathers or mothers, a receiver's spiritual covering, leaders of the ministry where the receiving person is planted. "It is like precious oil poured on the head, running down on the beard, running down on Aaron's beard, down on the collar of his robe" (Psalm 133:2). This Old Testament passage is a picture of how the anointing flows from the head down to the rest of the body.

An anointed vessel may impart the anointing to others in one or more of these different ways:

- *By the laying of hands*: "Do not neglect your gift, which was given you through prophecy when the body of elders laid their hands on you" (1 Timothy 4:14).
- *By pouring oil on the head*: "So Samuel took the horn of oil and anointed him in the presence of his brothers, and from that day on the Spirit of the Lord came powerfully upon David" (1 Samuel 16:13).
- *By declaring words of impartation, such as "I release this anointing to you"*: "While Peter was still speaking these words, the Holy Spirit came on all who heard the message" (Acts 10:44).

Just as the baptism of the Holy Spirit came upon people just through words spoken by anointed vessels like Peter, the anointing can be released through a vessel's words. This can happen when you are at a service where an anointed vessel is ministering, or it can happen while you are watching such ministry online. It can even happen when you are reading a book by an anointed minister and receiving the words declared (or written) in it. If you are surrendered to God and humble, you can be receiving an impartation of the anointing to walk in God's power right now, while you are reading these pages!

We are the Body of Christ, and we are made to work together as a Body. We are not meant to be separate; we need one another to function as one Body to the highest degree, so the Kingdom of God can expand effectively. God has created this system of the anointing's flow from one vessel to another so that we need each other and so that there is accountability and order. When we get into alignment with the proper order and flow of the anointing, there will not be misuse. You don't find Elisha, Joshua and Timothy misusing the anointing and having power trips and moral failures. You see them stewarding the anointing beautifully and pleasing God.

## DIFFERENT TYPES OF ANOINTING

God has different types of anointing that He releases for His different assignments. He gives the head of a ministry a specific vision. God then releases special anointing on the leader to complete that vision. He then brings many more vessels to help the leader accomplish that vision. The leader releases that same specific anointing to those who were brought to carry out the vision. The specific anointing is distributed widely to many to fully accomplish the vision, transcending generations. Moses didn't reach the Promised Land himself, but his anointing was released to Joshua. Joshua and those under Joshua's leadership were able to fulfill the vision that God had given Moses.

God also releases different anointings in different seasons, according to what His plans are. There was an evangelical anointing released to Billy Graham. In that time, God simply wanted the Gospel message to be preached so souls would be birthed into the Kingdom. God wanted His people to be saved and spiritual babies to be born to fill His churches. There then became a great need for pastors, and we saw the pastoral ministry rise up, as well as the teachers. We have seen mostly pastoral, teaching and evangelical anointings in the Body of Christ in recent decades. Because this is mostly all we have seen in recent Church history, most people don't even know that there are two other extremely important ministries in the Body of Christ: the apostles and the prophets. These two are actually the foundation of the Church, according to Ephesians 2:19–20: "Consequently, you are no longer foreigners and strangers, but fellow citizens with God's people and also members of his household, built on the foundation of the apostles and prophets, with Christ Jesus himself as the chief cornerstone" (Ephesians 2:19–20).

The devil has worked hard to get the Church to kick out its own foundation. These days, when most Christians hear *prophets*, they think *false prophets*. It is a doctrine of the devil to see a prophet with skepticism rather than as a gift to the Body of Christ. The Word of God tells us this: "Now these are the gifts Christ gave to the church: the apostles, the prophets, the evangelists, and the pastors and teachers" (Ephesians 4:11 NLT).

When many Christians hear *apostles*, they think, *There are no apostles left today*. Immediately, people judge true apostles and say they need to repent for "falsely" calling themselves an apostle. This is also a doctrine of the devil. The Word goes on to say of apostles and prophets, as well as of evangelists, pastors and teachers,

> Their responsibility is to equip God's people to do his work and build up the church, the body of Christ. This will continue until we all come to such unity in our faith and knowledge of

God's Son that we will be mature in the Lord, measuring up to the full and complete standard of Christ.

Ephesians 4:12–13 NLT

Notice the words *This will continue* until we all come to the fullness of Jesus. We have not reached this fullness yet, and we won't reach it until Jesus returns for His prepared Bride. Those called into the five-fold ministry, including the apostles and prophets, are part of preparing the Bride. They are the ones who *equip* the Body of Christ. We need equippers, leaders, those who release the spiritual nutrients and impartation that we all need! We will be spiritually lacking if we don't have all five of these offices operating in the Body.

## RESTORING THE FIVE-FOLD FOUNDATION

Now that God has had seasons of releasing evangelical, pastoral and teaching anointings, He is releasing the apostolic and prophetic anointings. We have entered the end-time revival. Jesus is not coming back until the Bride is fully prepared, "That he might present it to himself a glorious church, not having spot, or wrinkle, or any such thing; but that it should be holy and without blemish" (Ephesians 5:27 KJV). "Let us rejoice and be glad and give Him glory! For the wedding of the Lamb has come, and his bride has made herself ready" (Revelation 19:7). There are currently huge missing pieces of the Body of Christ because we are missing integral parts of the foundation. It's no wonder that when the foundation is missing, the power of God is rare.

Paul says, "The signs of a true apostle were performed among you . . . with signs and wonders and mighty works" (2 Corinthians 12:12 ESV). The *apostle* is the five-fold office that these signs, wonders and mighty works are a mark of, so it's no wonder that God's power in the Church is rare today, when the part of the foundation whose markers are miracles is cut out. The apostle is one of the major offices that imparts anointing and equips others to walk in miracles. We are also all called to prophesy, but by and large we don't see the Body of Christ operating in the prophetic. How could you expect the rest of the Body to be able to see when you eliminate the eye of the Body, the prophets? We need prophets, and apostles with prophetic anointing, to release prophetic anointing to the rest of the Body. The anointing flows from the head to the edge of the robes.

The church I pastor is called Five-Fold Church (5F Church). God gave us that name because He is now restoring the five-fold ministry to the Body of Christ. We have entered the end-time revival, where God is restoring the apostolic and prophetic ministries to the Body of Christ, so that the Church will be complete, lacking nothing.

I am an apostle, with apostolic and prophetic anointing. My spiritual father is a prophet, and I received this assignment to carry revival and restore the five-fold ministry through impartation from him. Other people whom God calls to help fulfill the assignment God gave me will receive this impartation of prophetic and apostolic anointing, too, whether they hold one of the five-fold offices or are another vessel in the Body of Christ. This doesn't mean that everyone will be apostles and prophets, but rather they will operate in the apostolic and prophetic anointing within their personal calling. It means that evangelists, pastors and teachers will also receive a prophetic anointing to minister prophetically within their offices. It means those ministries also have the heart for God's current move, and that all five offices and the rest of the Body of Christ work together to see this assignment accomplished.

For example, some evangelists who have not heard the call of God to restore the fivefold ministry into the Body may not understand the importance of the apostolic and prophetic ministries or have a heart for them. Many evangelists today only focus on reaching the lost and don't see the importance of maturing and discipling the spiritual babies born into the Kingdom. But there are evangelists who are called to this greater vision of fulfilling the fivefold ministry in today's Church. They still operate as evangelists, where their main gifting is to reach the unsaved and birth souls into the Kingdom. Yet they also have a greater understanding of what is needed to equip the saints. They have compassion for those babies to then receive apostolic and prophetic ministry so they can grow to be strong vessels of God, instead of being babies who die because of lack of nutrients, defeated by the devil because they never grow up spiritually.

I have seen evangelist-type Christians criticize the ministries of the apostles and prophets because their ministries look different. Evangelists tend to preach a similar message of salvation every time, whereas apostles and prophets teach messages that disciple and mature the spiritual babies. People are still being saved as the power of God works through these vessels, but it looks different from the typical structure of evangelical ministry in the Church by and large today, which is to preach the salvation message and do an altar call, with a "repeat after me" prayer for people who are raising their hands.

Paul said, "My message and my preaching were not with wise and persuasive words, but with a demonstration of the Spirit's power" (1 Corinthians 2:4). As Paul preached and ministered, the power of God was moving through him and people were having encounters with Jesus. As I minister, so many times I see the power of God touch people. Many times, they are healed and delivered, and then on their own they start weeping and yelling out, *Lord, I give my life to you! Jesus, I surrender!*

Evangelists called to this vision of the fivefold ministry fully operating in the Church are like Philip the Evangelist, who operated alongside the other four offices and understood that we all need each other and are all vital to the Body of Christ. Other believers who are not called to hold a fivefold office will still be called by God to help fulfill His vision of the complete fivefold ministry's restoration so that His fullness flows through the Body of Christ.

Those whom God calls to this vision will have a heart for revival. They will be done with dead churches bound by religion, and they will be hungry to encounter God's power and see others encounter His power, too. Those He calls to this vision will be childlike and humble, open to see Him moving in new ways. They will be able to adapt to God's will when it is different from their own will. Those God calls to this vision will be of every age, both male and female, new and old believers alike.

## APOSTOLIC ANOINTING

Webster defines an *apostle* as "one sent on a mission."* Apostles are "sent ones." This meaning comes from the Old English *apostol*, via ecclesiastical Latin, from the Greek *apostolos*, meaning "messenger," and from *apostellein*, meaning "send forth." Apostles are sent to preach the Gospel, heal the sick, cast out demons, raise the dead. All of us are called to this, but the apostles lead the way. These "sent ones" jump-start revival. They are the pioneers. They have zeal, passion and boldness to spread the Gospel and see people encounter God's power. They lay the foundation. Religion creeps into the Body of Christ, and apostles are always needed to pioneer revival and get the foundation to be pure and in line with God's will. When you receive apostolic anointing, you not only receive an anointing to walk in miracles; you also receive this "revival-starting" anointing. You receive an anointing to pioneer and start revival fires wherever you are. You receive an anointing that attracts people

---

*Merriam-Webster*, s.v. "apostle," accessed December 8, 2022, https://www.merriam-webster.com/dictionary/apostle.

to the revival fire within you, so they will encounter Jesus as they encounter you.

As the "sent ones" who serve as the foundation of the Church, apostles have a special grace to operate in all the fivefold giftings, especially in the beginnings of pioneering a church, when there is not yet every fivefold office present. Why were all twelve of Jesus' first disciples called apostles? Why was there not a prophet, evangelist, pastor and teacher among them? The reason is that the first disciples were all "pioneers" who walked in a grace to start the work of God and operate in all five giftings when the other four had not come yet. Once the apostles began the work of God, we saw the other offices of ministry soon joining them in the work of God. Philip was called the Evangelist; Agabus, Judas and Silas were prophets; Barnabas, Simeon, Lucius of Cyrene and Manaen were teachers (see Acts 13:1; 15:32; 21:8, 10).

Peter is one example of an apostle operating in the other fivefold ministry gifts. His first sermon was evangelical; three thousand people believed in Jesus in one day after hearing the Gospel message Peter preached (see Acts 2:41). Paul is another example. As an apostle, he shared that the most important spiritual gift to desire is the gift of prophecy: "Follow the way of love and eagerly desire gifts of the Spirit, especially prophecy" (1 Corinthians 14:1). From these examples we can see that as part of the Body of Christ's foundation, apostles must be prophetic and carry prophetic gifts/anointing to impart to others. Apostles always carry prophetic anointing, but they do so especially when no prophet is present in a church in the beginnings of its pioneering. God can grace an apostle with a strong prophetic gift in that case so nothing is lacking in the Body. That way, there are spiritual eyes that can discern God's will and also see where the enemy is hiding.

A big role of an apostle is to teach believers, so the teaching gifting is already part of the office of an apostle: "They devoted themselves to the apostles' teaching . . ." (Acts 2:42). Also, if the office of pastor is not present in a church, an apostle can operate in a pastoral gift so that the Body's pastoral needs are met. Apostles were operating pastorally in Acts 2:42–47, where we see those in the Church meeting together in harmony and being cared for as sheep.

An apostle also carries the grace to anoint all five offices of ministry and to impart all the gifts and anointing that vessels will need to walk in those offices. The same is true of prophets, since apostles and prophets serve as the foundation of the Church. For example, when God wants to anoint an evangelist in this move of God, an impartation to be in the office to evangelize can be released through me as an apostle. I can also impart apostolic and prophetic anointings as secondary giftings. When your spiritual father or mother is an apostle or prophet, he or she carries the grace to impart to you whatever is needed for your calling. If you are called to be a pastor, evangelist or teacher, for example, through the impartation of your spiritual father or mother who is an apostle or prophet, you will receive the anointing necessary to carry out your calling.

## PROPHETIC ANOINTING

Prophets speak a new, present-tense word of God. This word is for the edification and encouragement of believers. The prophetic word is a way that God speaks to His people. Receiving a prophetic word opens up a person's spiritual eyes to the incredible love of God, His nearness and His faithfulness. A prophetic word can also be a word of direction from God, or it can be about someone's calling (for example as a fivefold minister), or it can speak God's will for a person's life. Directional words and major words speaking God's will are mostly given by prophets or by apostles who carry prophetic anointing. Yet remember that the Bible says we should all prophesy:

In the last days, God says, I will pour out my Spirit on all people.
Your sons and daughters will prophesy, your young men will
see visions, your old men will dream dreams.

Acts 2:17

Let love be your highest goal! But you should also desire the special abilities the Spirit gives—especially the ability to prophesy.

1 Corinthians 14:1 NLT

Receiving prophetic words in my life opened up my eyes to
God's intimate love for me like never before. When I first received prophetic words, this knowing came where I just *knew*
God loved me—intimately *me*—for the first time! Upon hearing
those prophetic words, I *knew* that He was with me always,
that His plans for me were good, that I could trust Him and
that His Word really is true. Before that, I had believed in all
these things, but upon hearing this prophetic word, my spiritual
eyes opened up and I now *knew*. I felt close to God like never
before, and I have never been the same since. The directional
and edifying prophetic words I have received have opened my
eyes more to God's love for me. They have set me on the path of
His true will, where I felt rest, certainty and peace that I really
was in His will and was no longer wandering.

We are all called to be prophetic, to carry God's voice to
edify others. When you receive prophetic anointing (usually
through the impartation of a prophet or an apostle with prophetic anointing), the prophetic gift in you is activated. When
you receive the baptism of the Holy Spirit, you receive spiritual gifts. But when anointing comes upon you, the gifts are
unlocked. When you receive prophetic anointing, the prophetic
gift will work in you as you edify, encourage and pray for others.
You will speak to someone exactly what God needs him or her
to hear. When you receive true prophetic impartation, the gift
will work naturally (not forcefully), and with faith.

We shouldn't "try" to prophesy without God's leading. We shouldn't try to prophesy out of impure motives like trying to look spiritually impressive, or trying to feel good about ourselves as being very "spiritual." With a pure heart, we should encourage people with the love of God and pray for people with His heart. As you do this, the prophetic anointing will naturally flow from you as you step out in faith.

For example, as you are praying for someone, something specific might come to your mind. It may not be an audible voice or a vision, but you may just have a thought cross your mind that aligns with God's heart for the edification of the person. It doesn't have to be something highly detailed like knowing someone's phone number or address to be a prophetic word. The important thing is that God gets His message across, not how spiritually impressive a word sounds.

Sometimes, however, a prophetic word will be very detailed and will make someone go, "Wow! How did you know that?" That is for God's glory, to reveal that He really knows and loves the person. Yet something God has taught me is that it doesn't have to be highly detailed to be prophetic and be a word from God.

For example, someone might be going through a hard time where they don't feel seen or special. They feel as though they blend in and don't stand out. They keep getting doors shut in their faces and feel unnoticed and unimportant. But as you encourage and pray for such a person, God may lead you to say, "You are such a bright light! Like a star! You shine so brightly for Jesus and are so beautifully unique! God's anointing is upon you, and you are so needed and valuable in this world." You might think you're just saying a general word that can apply to everyone, but actually that word was prophetic and was exactly what God wanted that person to hear. In the moment, now the person *knows* it is God speaking directly to him or her.

When you receive prophetic anointing, whether to be a five-fold minister or to fulfill a different calling in the Body of Christ, you now have spiritual eyes to see. It doesn't mean you will necessarily see visions or visibly see angels and demons; it means there is a prophetic gifting where God is showing you things in the spiritual realm. Many times it may be a "knowing," or a thought that is actually God speaking. But in whatever way it comes, it is for the purpose of edifying the Body of Christ and revealing God's love and nearness to people.

## EVANGELIST, PASTORAL AND TEACHING ANOINTINGS

Evangelists, pastors and teachers can all be spiritual fathers and mothers and release impartation to others as well. Evangelists carry an anointing to reach the lost and birth souls into the Kingdom. Pastors carry the anointing to shepherd the sheep. They have a grace to care for people's personal issues in life. They have a grace to help the sheep be fed properly and help them stay in the house of God, not run away and get lost. Teachers carry an anointing to understand the Word of God and help believers hear God's voice in His Word. This anointing helps people grow spiritually.

Pastors, evangelists and teachers carry the anointing to impart to other pastors, evangelists and teachers, and to impart to other members of the Body of Christ. Only apostles and prophets carry the grace to anoint all five offices of ministry and impart all the gifts and anointing needed to minister in those offices. This is because, as we saw earlier, apostles and prophets are the foundation of the Body of Christ, with Christ Jesus as the chief cornerstone (see again Ephesians 2:19–20). So if you are called to be an apostle or prophet and God is calling you to receive impartation, you would need to receive it from an apostle or a prophet.

God has different assignments for different people, but it all has to do with advancing His Kingdom. God gave Elijah a vision, and when Elijah's time on earth was ending, God then called Elisha to help carry and fulfill this vision. Be open to whatever God's assignment is for you. Many times when God gives someone visions and dreams, those are fulfilled after that person helps fulfill a vision God gave someone else. Elisha walked in signs, wonders and miracles because he first obeyed when God told him to serve Elijah. If you have visions that God will do many miracles through you, it doesn't always mean you are to start a ministry immediately. Many times, the journey to reach the vision God gave you begins with serving another vessel or ministry operating in miracles. That is the way anointing is released to you to see your dream come to pass.

Pay attention to where God is impressing on your heart a certain passion. Is God impressing on you a passion to see others delivered and healed? Follow the leading of the Holy Spirit to where God's move of deliverance and healing is, and position yourself there to receive the anointing you need to help carry out this work of God.

If your passion is to evangelize, ask God where He is calling you to receive. He may be calling you to be positioned under another evangelist, or He may be calling you to bring your passion and gifting to a fivefold ministry church and be under an apostle or prophet to bring fullness to that work of God. Be sensitive to the Holy Spirit and ask Him, *Lord, what work of yours do you want me to be part of? Where is the place you have ordained for me to receive anointing and be equipped?*

As you surrender to God and seek His direction, I declare God's perfect will to be done in your life. May your steps be ordered by the Lord, and may there be peace and confirmation for who your "Elijah" is—the servant of God you will help, and who will impart anointing to you.

# 7

# How to Receive Impartation

Do not neglect the spiritual gift you received through the prophecy spoken over you when the elders of the church laid their hands on you.

1 Timothy 4:14 NLT

I traveled to my spiritual father's church in Tanzania about nine months after starting 5F Church, in March 2018. I was so expectant to receive an impartation of anointing. I was so hungry to see the power of God move at 5F Church and beyond. At that point, there were about twenty people in the church. I was preaching regularly and praying for people. I hadn't really seen the power of God move or seen any miracles happen yet. One time when I was praying for someone, she teared up. But that was the closest to the manifest power of God that I had seen.

I came to that church service at *Ngurumo ya Upako* church (Swahili for "The Roar of the Anointing") more expectant than ever before. I had received prophetic words that God would do many miracles through my life. I was so hungry for God to use me in that way so people could encounter His power and have a revelation of His love, just as had happened to me when the encounters I had set me on fire for Jesus.

During the church service in Tanzania, my spiritual father, Prophet Dr. GeorDavie, called me to the stage and began to prophesy and anoint me. As he poured oil on my head, I felt the power of God push me and I fell to the ground. He didn't even touch me. This was the first time I had experienced that. After that moment, I was brimming with excitement for the power of God to move at my church. Two people from my spiritual father's church, one an apostle and the other a prophet, drove me to the airport. They were telling me how it would be so different when I got back home, and how miracles would happen as I ministered. They spoke from their own experience after receiving impartation.

As I flew back to Los Angeles on the 23-hour plane ride, I immediately knew I was different. I usually would watch movies on the plane, but this time I had a hunger for God like I had never experienced. The entire flight I prayed and read the Bible. And when I read the Bible, I received revelation of the Word of God like never before in my life. I was amazed!

The first Sunday after returning to LA, I was so hungry and expectant for the power of God to move. About fifteen people were at church that day. After I preached, I started praying for a woman. God gave me words for her, and as I spoke them she began weeping. In that moment, I knew that the prophetic anointing had come upon me. This was the first time I had ever experienced that. I then went to pray for someone else, and that person went down to his knees and began to weep. I prayed for another person, and the same thing happened. God was giving me personal words for people for the very first time.

Jeanntal had not yet come to 5F Church at this point. She would arrive just two weeks after this, and then later would join me as a ministry partner. But on this day, her mother,

Viviane, came for the first time. As I prayed for her I touched her hand lightly, and as I did, the power of God pushed her back and she fell to the ground. I was shocked. I had seen this happen and had experienced it myself as my spiritual father ministered. But I had never seen the power of God move through me like this. I was in awe. In this moment, I knew for sure I had received impartation and the anointing was moving through me.

From that day on, the power of God would move regularly, through prophetic ministry, through baptisms in the Holy Spirit, and through the anointing touching people so mightily that they could no longer remain on their feet. For the next four years the church decreased in numbers, but the power of God continued to move. Because of the small numbers, it did not look or feel like revival, but I was so grateful for the power of God continually moving and touching people, giving them revelation that He loved them so much.

I had faith that the anointing imparted to me was growing and that one day I would see the shocking miracles that were prophesied take place. And indeed God was faithful, and His promises came to pass. The anointing has grown so much. Now, sometimes even as I am preaching, demons tremble and come out of people, even without prayer. God does so many miracles! At every Sunday service at 5F Church or revival service I hold elsewhere, He heals and delivers several people, whether they have come in person or are viewing a service online.

## BE PLANTED

The story of Elijah and Elisha carries so much revelation that applies to us today on how to receive an impartation of anointing. Elijah was a prophet who walked in such powerful anointing. He was raising the dead, healing the sick, bringing fire down from heaven and making the rain fall. After Elijah left earth and was taken up to heaven, Elisha received Elijah's mantle (see 2 Kings 2). *Mantle* in the spiritual realm means the specific anointing that someone carries. When Elisha received Elijah's mantle, he received the same anointing and grace as Elijah had. We see Elisha do the same mighty miracles that Elijah did and more—in fact, double.

The first thing to notice about this impartation is that Elisha received all his anointing from God through Elijah. It wasn't from here, there and everywhere. He didn't receive the anointing from multiple people. He had all the anointing he needed through that impartation of one person (and actually double). Here's a secret about impartation that goes against Western "buffet culture": *The secret to walking in powerful anointing is to be planted under one ministry where the anointing is flowing from the head.*

Remember the verse we looked at earlier: "It is like precious oil poured on the head, running down on the beard, running down on Aaron's beard, down on the collar of his robe" (Psalm 133:2). The anointing flows from the top of the head, down the beard, to the edges of the robe. The head in this verse represents the head/leader of an anointed ministry. The rest of the body—the beard, the edges of the robe and every other part of the body in between—are the believers who plant themselves in that ministry. When you plant yourself, you are literally positioning yourself to receive anointing. You are positioning yourself where the anointing is flowing. If you are not under the waterfall, you are not getting wet. But if you are simply standing under the waterfall, you are getting drenched. You are immersed. You are completely covered and continually filled to overflowing with the water. This is how it is with receiving an impartation of anointing.

What does being planted look like? For one thing, being planted means to be receiving consistently through the ministry

God called you to be planted in. "That person is like a tree planted by streams of water, which yields its fruit in season and whose leaf does not wither—whatever they do prospers" (Psalm 1:3). God gave gifts to the Church so that believers would be edified and would receive the proper spiritual nutrients and food to grow into mature vessels of God—victorious over the enemy, walking in the power of God and now able to make disciples themselves: "Therefore go and make disciples of all nations, baptizing them in the name of the Father and of the Son and of the Holy Spirit, and teaching them to obey everything I have commanded you" (Matthew 28:19–20; see also Ephesians 4:11–16).

This is God's system of equipping and strengthening His Body. This is the real Church! This is why it's so important to be planted, to be continually receiving this equipping and the flow of the anointing. When you are being equipped and taught, you're not receiving head knowledge like the knowledge of this world that you learn going to college. You're receiving spiritual food. Paul talks about giving spiritual food to his disciples: "I gave you milk, not solid food, for you were not yet ready for it. Indeed, you are still not ready" (1 Corinthians 3:2). As you are planted week after week, you are receiving anointed teaching. You are receiving things in the spirit that are making you become more spiritual and less carnal. Just positioning yourself to receive (attending a true anointed church or ministry, whether online or in person), makes impartation come upon you when your heart is trustworthy to receive anointing.

The impartation to walk in the power of God comes first when He sees your heart is trustworthy, as we talked about in chapter 3. And then, when your heart is seen as trustworthy, God will in most cases lead you to the vessel from which you will receive the anointing. The teaching you receive in such a ministry equips you to properly steward and use the anointing, and to overcome the enemy's schemes against God's anointed ones. The teaching also disciples you to be a mature, anointed vessel of God and equips you to disciple others. Every time you are positioned under that waterfall of anointing, the anointing is flowing to you. You are receiving more and more of it, and as you remain planted, God sees you as more and more trustworthy to carry even more anointing.

This way of being planted is Kingdom culture, but it is definitely not Western culture. In a world of many different streaming services, social media platforms, tons of restaurant options, stores, cars, etc., we are very much a buffet culture. That buffet culture has seeped into the Body of Christ. There are many amazing, anointed vessels of God in the Body, but we are not called to treat every ministry or minister as just one option out of many that we choose off a spiritual buffet that we go to once in a while. Rather, we are called to be planted in one place.

When you are planted in a place where true anointing is, you're not missing out because of not going to five different Bible studies or different church services a week. Doing church buffet style can be okay for a season—perhaps when you are hungry and are on a journey to find out where God wants you to be planted. You have to seek, and for a season the seeking may take you to many different places, until you find the place God wants you planted: "You will seek me and find me when you seek me with all your heart" (Jeremiah 29:13). But once God has led you to that place, just stay. Don't remove yourself from underneath the waterfall! This is your moment. You have found your "Elijah." If you treat this Elijah leader as just an option on the buffet, you will never receive the anointing, as Elisha did:

> So he departed from there, and found Elisha the son of Shaphat, who was plowing with twelve yoke of oxen before him, and he was with the twelfth. Then Elijah passed by him and threw his

mantle on him. And he left the oxen and ran after Elijah, and said, "Please let me kiss my father and my mother, and then I will follow you."

And he said to him, "Go back again, for what have I done to you?"

So Elisha turned back from him, and took a yoke of oxen and slaughtered them and boiled their flesh, using the oxen's equipment, and gave it to the people, and they ate. Then he arose and followed Elijah, and became his servant.

1 Kings 19:19–21 NKJV

Once God called Elisha to be planted under Elijah, God wanted Elisha immediately to leave everything. When God speaks to you, *This is where I want you to be planted*, He will ask you to be serious about it and to make room in your life to be planted. This will mean leaving some things behind and saying good-bye to some people who just were not called to be the ones beside you for every season. When you are obedient in letting go of those whom God is asking you to, you are making room for God to put beside you those who will help you reach your calling. David had Jonathan, who loved him like himself. God used Jonathan to help David reach his promised land. In addition to your "Elijah," there are "Jonathans" God is ready to release to you, once you obey Him and make room for them.

## MAINTAIN A SERVANT HEART

When God called Elisha to be planted under Elijah, He also called Elisha to serve Elijah. Elijah's life was serving God and doing the work He had called him to. It was a big job, and God called Elisha to help Elijah carry out the work. When Elisha was serving Elijah, he was directly serving God, because Elijah's whole life was serving God, and what God had called him to do was too big to accomplish alone, without others serving and helping make the work to go forth. Elijah was given the massive vision and assignment, and Elisha was called to help Elijah carry out that vision and assignment.

Elisha's whole assignment was to serve Elijah with whatever he needed. God wanted Elisha to stay firmly planted under Elijah, continually serving him. On one occasion, Elijah says to Elisha that he can stay somewhere while Elijah goes on to Bethel, and later, he tells Elisha to stay when he goes to Jericho. Both times, Elisha says no, he will not leave Elijah:

> Elijah said to Elisha, "Stay here; the LORD has sent me to Bethel."
> But Elisha said, "As surely as the LORD lives and as you live, I will not leave you." So they went down to Bethel.
> The company of the prophets at Bethel came out to Elisha and asked, "Do you know that the LORD is going to take your master from you today?"
> "Yes, I know," Elisha replied, "so be quiet."
> Then Elijah said to him, "Stay here, Elisha; the LORD has sent me to Jericho."
> And he replied, "As surely as the LORD lives and as you live, I will not leave you." So they went to Jericho.
>
> 2 Kings 2:2–4

This was actually a test for Elisha. God was testing him to see if his heart was truly trustworthy enough to carry the powerful mantle of Elijah. God was testing whether or not Elisha was truly obedient and loyal. He passed the test when he refused to leave Elijah.

We are also called to be servants of God and His people. The Bible says, "Anyone who wants to be first must be the very last, and the servant of all" (Mark 9:35). God needs to test that in us. The way He tests us and our humility to see if we are servant-hearted enough to put God and others before ourselves is by seeing if we will serve others faithfully and continually.

The purpose of the anointing is to carry out the precious work of God. The anointing is 100 percent the power of Jesus working through us, which is Jesus Himself. The anointing is not some special superpower outside Jesus that someone gets. It is 100 percent Jesus. When we see an anointed vessel ministering, we should not look at the person, but at Jesus. We should praise and give glory to Him alone.

Unfortunately, some people see an anointed vessel and look at the person more than they look at Jesus. Some people think, *I want that power so I can look important and powerful, and build my "empire."* These people will be the ones who don't rejoice when someone is delivered and healed. They are missing the beautiful miracle that *Jesus* alone did, where a person went from suffering to freedom, from pain or sickness to health, from death to life, from not knowing God's love to meeting Jesus. Instead, these observers are looking only at the anointed vessel of God with eyes of jealousy, thinking, *I want that.*

Jealousy always leads to hate. It always opens doors to the devil speaking lies about another person. This is what made King Saul go on a mission to kill David. He couldn't find joy in God using David to defeat many more enemies than ever before, even though this was a blessing for Saul and his whole kingdom. He forgot how God used David to bless him by playing the harp, casting demons out of him. Instead, all Saul could see was, *David has more power than I do, and I don't like that! I want to be more powerful than David. I want what he has. I want to push him down so he's not looking more powerful than I look!*

True anointed vessels don't see themselves in that nature at all. They are humble servants. They have sacrificed so much, not so they could get power, but purely out of obedience to God. They see themselves as slaves to Christ, as the apostle Paul did: "This letter is from Paul, a slave of Christ Jesus, chosen by God to be an apostle and sent out to preach his Good News" (Romans 1:1 NLT).

Anointed vessels are so busy being servants of God and giving every ounce of themselves to Him that there isn't even time to think of their own desires, only His. They humble themselves regularly to remind themselves that it's only by God's grace that they are anointed. They remember always that they are not entitled to be anointed or have any of the blessings that come with anointing. The whole "looking powerful and important" mindset is not in the hearts of true anointed vessels whom God chooses. They don't see themselves as more important than others. They see themselves as servants of others and see that they have been blessed to bless others. "Heal the sick, raise the dead, cleanse those who have leprosy, drive out demons. *Freely you have received; freely give*" (Matthew 10:8, emphasis added).

When we see an anointed minister, we should just see Jesus and be so happy that He is moving in power through someone. We should praise God that people are encountering His love and being delivered and healed. When we truly have a heart for God's people, we don't care how a person is saved, healed and delivered. Our heart says, *I don't care whom God uses with mighty anointing, whether it's an ex-murderer like the apostle Paul, someone whose personality I'm not a fan of, my favorite minister or me—I don't care. Male, female, young, old, lots of experience in ministry or not, I don't care. I just want God to have His way!*

That is the heart God can anoint. That is the heart that has no problem serving an anointed minister. We should be so excited that anointing is here among us that we want to do all we can to be part of making the revival spread and making God's work go forth. We shouldn't have a heart that says, *I want to start my own ministry* (out of selfish ambition, not God's will), or *I want to be powerful*, or *I want to look spiritual* or *I want to have many followers*. Our heart should be, *Lord, I want to serve you, whatever it looks like. Whatever way I can help advance the Kingdom of God, that's what I want to do!*

This is the heart of Elisha. God tests this heart in you as He asks you to serve your "Elijah"—the anointed minister whom He has called you to be planted under. He tests your heart to see if you care about finding fame and a platform, or if you truly just want to see God be glorified and His Kingdom be advanced in whatever way He wants to do it.

Many believers miss out on carrying the anointing because they are too prideful and jealous of a minister to serve their "Elijah." The devil loves to send those jealous thoughts our way, just as he did to King Saul. If you accept the jealousy spirit, you will most likely try to "kill" the ministry you are jealous of by speaking and acting against it. You also will not only be attacking an anointed vessel of God; you will literally be an agent of Satan. This is a very strategic scheme of the enemy against every anointed minister. It is the same spirit the Pharisees had, who didn't like that Jesus was attracting bigger crowds than they did, so they ended up doing everything in their power to kill Him and His ministry. It was the "people of God" who killed Jesus and tried to kill God's work.

Today, it is once again the "people of God" who let jealousy come into their hearts. What if we were all united, and we all rejected every spirit of jealousy? Instead of attacking each other, we could actually be a team, a united Body, defeating the devil's works and advancing the Kingdom of God in greater ways than we have ever seen. "Humble yourselves before the Lord, and he will lift you up in honor" (James 4:10 NLT).

If you have found yourself battling with jealous thoughts, know that you don't have to receive those jealous lies of the devil. Jealousy begins with the devil speaking lies and trying to make you think they are your own thoughts, that you *are* jealous. This is the devil's scheme to steal, kill and destroy—to try to kill your future serving God and to try to kill an anointed vessel's ministry through you. Don't let the devil win! God is calling you to be anointed. God is calling you to serve your

Elijah. What would have happened if Elisha was too jealous and prideful to serve Elijah? He would not have received the anointing. Renew your mind about this truth.

Many times the people you're jealous of are the ones who are called to bless you and release the anointing to you to make your God-given dreams come true. They might even be called to release a double portion of the anointing that they have to you, just as Elisha received double from Elijah. How horrible it would be to miss out on God's beautiful blessings and the calling on your life to walk in mighty anointing, because you refuse to humble yourself.

Give any jealous thoughts to God. Take every thought captive to Christ (see 2 Corinthians 10:5). "Resist the devil, and he will flee from you" (James 4:7). Reject the lies of the devil with your mouth. Speak out loud, "Every jealous lie must go. I love and bless _____ " (the person you hear jealous lies about from the devil). Pray for that person. If he or she is your Elijah, serve that minister. Ask how you can help, how you can serve. Tell the person that you're blessed that God uses him or her and that you want to help the work of God go forth.

Intentionally speak good about this minister to others, rather than gossip. If people are gossiping about the person, whether online or in person, choose to speak positively about him or her instead. Avoid watching negative videos other jealous people have made to attack ministers. Such videos can be found about every anointed minister of today. Making these videos is a tactic of modern-day Pharisees. Humble yourself! Have God's thoughts and heart for this person you're tempted to become jealous of. Ask God to help you become more humble.

## HOW TO SERVE WITH EXCELLENCE

Now you know that one of the biggest keys to receiving impartation is to serve an anointed man or woman whom God is calling you to receive impartation from. Elisha was not just a follower of Elijah. He was not just a companion. First and foremost, he was Elijah's servant. He served God directly as he served Elijah. Every single day, he lived a life of servanthood, humbling himself in the position of a willing servant. He didn't have selfish ambition. He was content being Elijah's servant because he knew it was what God had called him to, and he just wanted to obey God.

Lazarus's sister Mary poured expensive perfume on Jesus' feet and wiped His feet with her hair. She was carrying out an important spiritual act of preparing Him for the crucifixion (see John 12:3, 7). We can take a powerful lesson from what she did. Above all, she was serving Jesus in this moment. She was lying prostrate as she wiped His feet with her hair, symbolizing surrender. She gave very expensive perfume, which symbolizes giving your all, all that is precious to you, to God and His work. And when she left Jesus' presence, she smelled just like Jesus. She wiped that perfume poured upon Him with her hair, and she carried that scent with her. As you serve the anointing, you will then "smell" like that same anointing you serve. Meaning, that anointing has become part of you. As you serve, that anointing is imparted into you.

Many people are distracted with their own ambitions and ministries, when God is asking them to be still and serve so the anointing can pour into their lives. Many miss this principle of impartation, and that's a big reason why anointing is rare. You cannot receive anointing by being anxious, only focusing on your own ambitions and being too busy to serve. Serving God is not a waste of time! Serving God is where His power is. Serving is the greatest use of your time and pleases Him so much! "If you are faithful in little things, you will be faithful in large ones. But if you are dishonest in little things, you won't be honest with greater responsibilities" (Luke 16:10 NLT).

Let's say you know that God is calling you to start a ministry. You need to be sensitive to when He's calling you to actually put things into motion for your ministry. Many times when God is calling a person to be a minister, some steps in how to get there are missed. God often speaks one's calling to be a minister, but may then want the called one to serve first, just like Elisha. It was God's calling for Elisha to have his own huge ministry. But for a long time, God was first calling Elisha to do nothing but serve Elijah. What would have happened if Elisha had left Elijah prematurely to start his own ministry? He would not have received the mantle!

I had never seen anyone walk in such a high level of anointing as my spiritual father. I also had never encountered God's love and power so much in my life as through the ministry of my spiritual father. I wanted the whole world to encounter God the way I had! For the first four years of ministering, I didn't see tons of miracles happen through me. There were some here and there, but nothing compared to the miracles that happened through my spiritual father. I had this heart of, *I want God to promote him to reach more people, so more people can encounter the power of God through him the way I have!*

I knew the prophecies over my life—that I was called to walk in God's power and reach the nations—but my heart was not like, *Oh, I can't wait to be just like my spiritual father!* I just had this simple desire for people to encounter the power of God, so I hungered for *his* ministry to reach more people, rather than "*my* ministry." It was being Kingdom-minded rather than being focused on myself or my ministry. It's good to want your ministry to succeed for God's glory, but unfortunately many people want their ministry to succeed for selfish ambitious reasons (wanting power, fame, success or money). I just had this single desire: *I want people to encounter Jesus in power and know His love!*

I served my spiritual father whenever God called me to, with whatever he needed help with. I took serving with excellence very seriously. I had the revelation that to serve a true anointed man or woman of God is really to serve God Himself—it is 100 percent the work of God. Elijah was doing such an important work of God with his life, and he couldn't do it all on his own. So when Elisha served Elijah, he was making the work of God go forth, and he was serving God directly. I knew it was God's will for me to receive the anointing, and I knew that serving was the way to receive. I knew this is what was pleasing to God.

God taught me these precious secrets to receiving anointing: *You cannot receive anointing if you don't have a servant heart through and through. You cannot receive anointing if you have selfish ambitions.*

God will ask you to serve in many different ways, in uncomfortable ways, in ways not your strength, in ways behind the scenes that no one sees. God will call you to deny yourself and put another person before yourself again and again. He will call you to serve while you are fighting the enemy's lies that say, *You should focus on your dream! Why are you wasting your time?* There will be people who don't understand what you're doing and think you're neglecting your own dreams as you spend time serving another. There will be many tests as you serve, testing whether you truly have a servant heart toward God and others.

When it comes to the work of God, there is so much to be done. We are the Body of Christ, and we are all called to do God's work. If some parts of the Body are not doing the work, then other parts of the Body have to take on more. For a very long time, I was doing most things in the ministry at 5F Church, and Jeanntal was the only one assisting me. Even before the video went viral and revival broke out in 2021, I would spend so much time doing work for the ministry. I would spend ten to twelve hours per day editing sermons (that would get just a few views), editing small preaching clips, going live and posting encouragement on social media. This was a burden I carried because of the lack of those serving. I know God took me through that season on purpose, to prepare me for even more work to be done, to stretch me to be even more surrendered as I worked hard and served Him with everything in me and to refine me through the fire.

It's important to realize that there is so much work to be done in a ministry. There are so many areas where you can lift a burden placed on another part of the body, and the Kingdom of God can then advance quicker and farther.

## GOD IS WAITING FOR YOU TO STEP UP

There is so much more work to be done in the Kingdom, and so many places to serve. God is just waiting for you to step up and serve! This is the case for many anointed ministries. There is so much to do, and the work is done as people serve and everyone in the Body takes their place.

When it comes to church services, remember that preaching the Gospel, healing the sick and casting out demons are not the only "works of God." There is so much that goes into reaching people and putting on a service with excellence. If every single one of us all at one time are preaching, who is inviting people? Who is using his or her creative gifts of outreach? Who is making a flyer so people know when and where the service will take place?

Someone just testified that God showed her a dream of a blue sky with birds, and she knew she would be delivered when she saw that picture. Then the graphic Jeanntal designed for the "Revival Is Now" event in this person's area was posted, and on the graphic were birds and a blue sky—exactly the same as in her dream. She knew she needed to attend the event, and that if she did, she would be set free. And Jesus did set her free there! Look how God used graphics for an event to speak to people and lead them to get delivered! But someone had to step up and serve by doing the work.

There were people who took time to record what Jesus did in the Bible. Who will record on camera what God is doing today? Who will edit the videos and post them so millions of people can encounter Jesus instead of just one hundred people there physically? Who will catch and care for the people who are being delivered? Who will help manage the crowd and maintain order since God is not a God of chaos, but order? Who will organize the revival service and make it possible for people to receive?

These are just a few examples of all the different kinds of "works of God." All are vital and important. We need the entire Body to play its part. We need every aspect of the work of God done with excellence, to reach the most people. God wants you to serve His servants because there is so much to do and He needs you! The more we serve and fill in every missing aspect, the more people will be saved and the Kingdom will advance.

How do you serve an anointed servant of God? Tell God you are ready to serve! When you make yourself available, He will open up doors and lead you to exactly where He wants you to serve. Many times, He will ask you to serve in the place where there is need. Ask the minister whom God is calling you to serve, "How can I help in the work of God? What do you need help with? How can I be a blessing to you and to the ministry?" If you are part of a ministry from afar, watching online, a big way you can serve is by sharing videos of the Word of God, miracles and testimonies. Invite your friends, family and co-workers to watch online and encounter Jesus. Use social media to spread the Good News. Share your testimony with as many people as possible and keep sharing it!

Serve with the revelation that you are serving God Himself. Serve with the revelation that you are pleasing God so much and that you are literally receiving anointing as you serve. You are receiving impartation to walk in the power of God, but also you are receiving the anointing in every area of your life, for all your needs. At one "Revival Is Now" service, a gentleman had volunteered to be one of my assistants during the time when I would be praying for people individually. He later told me that the same night he served, he dreamt that I prayed for him, placing my hand on his head and praying for his deliverance. When he awoke, the tormenting thoughts he'd had in his mind for as long as he could remember were completely gone. He told me, "I didn't know it was possible for these thoughts to just completely go away." He also visited one of his parents that day, whom he had held bitterness toward because of past trauma. When he visited, he felt a supernatural love for this parent, and forgiveness. He was amazed! This man was serving and got delivered while he was serving. When you are serving the anointing, you're positioned for the anointing to destroy yokes and heal you, and you're positioned to receive an impartation of that anointing.

When I started serving God in the anointing, I noticed that consequently I became more spiritual and more Christlike. It was simply a result of serving God. I was amazed to see how just being serious about God's business completely transformed my life. Jesus told us, "For my yoke is easy and my burden is light" (Matthew 11:30).

The anointing is so powerful that when you are immersed in it by serving, it flows so mightily in your life that it makes what used to be a struggle become easy. You don't have to try with your physical strength to be more Christlike. You will also see God's hand on your life like never before as you serve: doors opening, problems going away and abundance coming in every area of your life. Just by serving God in His work, I have seen Him provide for all my needs and open up supernatural door after supernatural door, taking me from a place of lack to overflowing abundance!

It's important to serve God in the work that needs doing, because the work needs to go on. But what's even more important to God is what happens spiritually as you serve. Your service is an act of surrender, an act of denying yourself. This is an act of putting God first by honoring a servant of God, which is honoring God Himself. Jesus told the disciples serving in His ministry, "Anyone who receives you receives me, and anyone who receives me receives the Father who sent me" (Matthew 10:40 NLT).

Purely the act of serving causes God to release anointing to you. Your serving results in God depositing anointing upon you—simply that. We could hire worldly people to edit, run cameras and do all the work that needs doing in the Church, but God really wants you to be the one serving. Why? Because (1) the work gets done by His anointed vessels, with anointing on the work, and (2) your heart can be transformed through serving, and God can entrust you with anointing. God wants you to serve because of what happens to you spiritually when you serve.

## SOW INTO GOD'S WORK

Here's another key to receiving impartation: *Sow into the anointing that you serve. God calls us all to sow into the work of God.* Most Christians know this and many Christians tithe, although many give with a limited revelation of their seed. Most Christians think their offering is helping the work of God go forth and that's it. So most Christians give because they want their physical money to help with the physical needs of the Church, and they also want to obey God because He instructs us to tithe.

But there is so much more that happens in the spiritual realm when you give, and give with revelation. "Do not be deceived, God is not mocked; for whatever a man sows, that he will also reap" (Galatians 6:7 NKJV). It's simple: *Whatever* you sow, you *will* reap. God gives us seed. You can choose to plant your seed in dry soil, but you will not reap spiritual blessings from that soil. If you sow seed into rich, healthy soil, however, with the perfect environment for a plant to grow, you will reap a healthy, beautiful harvest.

When you sow into true anointing, you will reap that anointing in your life. Jesus paid the price for you to receive abundant life (see John 10:10). But to receive that abundant life, you need to be receiving the fullness of Jesus who comes in power. Jesus who comes in power *is* the anointing. You need the power of God to break yokes of poverty and release abundant finances. You need the power of God to break generational curses of sickness and release abundant health. You need the power of God to cast out demons of anxiety, depression, suicidal thoughts and night terrors. You need the power of God to break the yoke of stagnancy and rejection and open supernatural doors for you. To receive the precious anointing in your life to walk in God's power, you need to sow into that anointing.

Why would you sow into bad soil and then pray to receive the anointing and expect it to come into your life? Again, whatever you sow, you will reap. Just as with serving, God doesn't want you to sow just so His Church can have the physical money to get the physical things needed for the ministry. Those are very important, but God wants you to give with the full revelation of the power of your seed. The main reason God wants you to give is because of what you receive spiritually when you give.

God wants your heart to be transformed into His, and He wants to release anointing to you. Sowing is one of the ways this happens. Money is important to every human because we need it to live. When you give to God, you are truly making a sacrifice. And making sacrifices is necessary in order for your heart to be transformed into the image of Christ. You cannot be fully surrendered without sacrificing and sacrificing continually. God may ask you to give amounts that are a real sacrifice. The greater the anointing, the greater the sacrifice. Through this, God is shaping your heart to be completely about His Kingdom, and void of your own selfish interests.

# 8

# Testimonies of Impartation

Sing to the LORD; praise his name. Each day proclaim the good news that he saves. Publish his glorious deeds among the nations. Tell everyone about the amazing things he does.

Psalm 96:2–3 NLT

It was only in the first month after the first demon had been cast out that I started hearing testimonies of impartation people received at 5F Church. One family was so hungry for God that they traveled to Los Angeles from the East Coast to come to a 5F Church service. One young man among them watched another family member be powerfully delivered. During that service, I released the anointing to be imparted to the crowd. I didn't lay hands to impart it; I just spoke the word. After this family returned to their home state, I received a testimony that the young man had prayed for some more of his family members shortly after he returned home. In each case, demons manifested and came out as he commanded them to leave. That had never happened to him before as he prayed. He received impartation at 5F Church, and God immediately began to use him.

We talked in chapter 3 about the cost of the anointing. Part of the cost sometimes may be to travel physically to be in a church service and receive the anointing, as this family did. When you make the sacrifice to travel to where the anointing is, there is a reward of impartation. Making such a sacrifice is a test of your surrender. Especially if you don't live near where God calls you to be planted, there will come a time when God asks you to make a sacrifice and travel in person to receive impartation. As I mentioned earlier, the first time I started noticing the power of God moving through me was after I had visited my spiritual father's church in person. I had already received the anointing and was receiving impartation from afar. But I received the greatest and most noticeable measure when I went in person.

I have heard many such testimonies from people who have been at one of my revival services across the world, or who have attended 5F Church in person (even if they now attend online). I want to share just a few of them with you. Some of these people received deliverance, and all of them received impartation because they became planted, they started sowing and serving, and they have humble hearts. As I got to know each of them, I could see the qualities they all shared—humility, childlikeness, and a selfless desire just to see God's people be free and encounter Him. As I saw the purity in their hearts, I could see why God entrusted them with the anointing.

## HEATHER'S IMPARTATION TESTIMONY

Heather Holley-Baeumel has loved Jesus for over forty years. She has attended and taught at Bible college, and she has served in many kinds of ministries, including praise and worship, children and youth, prayer and mentoring other women. She and her husband, Larry, are co-pastors of True Grace Church in

Redlands, California. Heather longed for the power of God to move in the church so people who were bound could be set free. Impartation was key! Here is Heather's story:

Last year, several people who were tormented by demons came through our church, and I realized I lacked the ability to minister deliverance effectively to them. I couldn't give them what I saw Jesus or His apostles had given people, so I began to cry out to God for more! I was desperate to see them experience the kind of freedom I read about in the Bible.

A few days after a time of prayer about this, I was tagged in a post from 5F Church on social media. Apostle Kathryn was ministering, and I was *amazed* at what I was seeing! God moved so mightily through this humble woman, driving out demons that had tormented people for years. I watched video after video and saw her doing exactly what I was believing God for in our church. I laughed because I hadn't expected God to bring me to a young woman apostle preaching in a park in downtown Los Angeles, but isn't it just like Him to bring answers in unusual ways?

One Sunday after our church service was over, I traveled a couple of hours to a 5F Church service in the park. I felt like Moses at the burning bush, God was speaking to me so strongly! I was captivated by His presence there. The entire experience was unlike anything I had ever encountered before.

As Apostle Kathryn ministered, I witnessed many demons coming out of people, many healings, and many people being filled with the Holy Spirit. I cried with joy as I saw the relief come to people! After three weeks of coming to 5F services every Sunday after our own service, I stepped up during ministry time and requested an impartation of the anointing. Apostle Kathryn laid hands on me and imparted the anointing (see 2 Timothy 1:6), and I felt it go into me! I fell under the power of the Holy Spirit.

Three days later, a demon manifested at our Wednesday night service. I was able to cast it out, and the woman was set free. I marveled that this power was now flowing in me. God had answered the prayers of my heart. No one had ever had a demon cast out at our church, and not many were healed. We were mainly a "teaching church," with little power. But now, *everything changed.* In every service since then, people have gotten delivered and healed so easily!

My husband saw this amazing ministry taking place and received deliverance himself through me. Soon, he wanted to go get impartation from Apostle Kathryn as well, so he drove to 5F Church and received it. Now, he regularly casts out demons and ministers deliverance to people. Several people have also been miraculously healed of all kinds of disease at our services, and the healings continue!

I have now begun to hold "Revival in the Park" services in our city every six weeks, and people are coming and receiving deliverance and healing as they listen to the Gospel. I continue to visit 5F Church and listen diligently to Apostle Kathryn's anointed teaching and preaching. I am being discipled and am learning so much as I sit at her feet. As she increases in the anointing, we all get the beautiful benefits, and I see myself increasing in the spirit of wisdom and revelation.

Our church is hungry for the things of God, and I look forward with great joy to the wonderful things He will do in our area and around the world. Our best days are right now! And I declare with a joyful shout, *Revival Is Now!*

## DEMAREE'S IMPARTATION TESTIMONY

Eighteen-year-old Demaree Carreon lives a few hours away from 5F Church. She attends in person whenever she can; otherwise, she tunes in to every service online. She serves diligently by sharing 5F's videos with as many people as possible, and she also helps edit videos for 5F Church. Demaree also faithfully sows into the work of God. Last year, she received impartation through a Zoom meeting I held and immediately started moving in the power of God and changing people's lives, starting with her own family. Here is Demaree's story:

I am planted at 5F Church virtually. When I was seventeen, Apostle Kathryn prayed for me on a Zoom meeting she held. Jesus set me free, and I encountered His love for the very first time. The moment I was set free, I said the words "I want people to know Him!" She then prophesied that God would do many miracles through me, and that many children and youth would receive miracles through me. She saw me leading a revival group at my school.

Shortly after that day, I made one hundred copies of flyers saying *Revival Is Now* and I put them all over my high school. I started a Bible study/Revival club at school, where I would preach to students and pray for them.

A few months after Apostle Kathryn prayed for me, a family member who didn't know Jesus told me about having bad dreams and becoming fearful. I prayed with the person, and demons started manifesting. They left when I commanded them to go! This was the very first time I saw God move in power through me. This family member literally felt Jesus' touch that day and now believes in Him.

From that day, I then started going live and praying for people on my livestream. Demons manifested in people and were cast out as I commanded them to go. Many people have been set free as I prayed for them. Every time I go live now, people are set free! One woman who attended my livestream wanted prayer for a skin condition. She began renouncing spiritually bad things in her life as God led her, and I declared her loosed from whatever she renounced. I also commanded every spirit of infirmity to leave her. She started coughing (which sometimes happens with deliverance), and then she said, "I feel so free!" A couple of days later, she sent me photos of herself in which she was completely free and clear of her skin condition. Hallelujah! I'm so in awe of the power of impartation. Just by positioning myself and planting myself where God's power is moving at 5F

Church, under Apostle Kathryn, I've seen the anointing move in my life and God do miracles through me that I never could've imagined!

## RICHARD'S IMPARTATION TESTIMONY

Richard Hislop is a 37-year-old evangelist from Virginia who would often see salvations and baptisms in the Holy Spirit whenever he preached and ministered, but who was not seeing any deliverances. He longed for God to use him to destroy the enemy's yokes so people could find freedom. After he and his wife attended a "Revival Is Now" event on the National Mall where I released an impartation of the anointing, God met the longing of his heart. Here is Richard's story:

> For years, I've yearned to see people set free. I've prayed that God would increase the anointing on my life so He could use me to the fullest in the work of the Great Commission—to cast out demons, heal the sick, raise the dead and free the oppressed. On seeing Apostle Kathryn's ministry, I longed even more to see people delivered.
>
> Last year, I attended a revival service at the National Mall in Washington, D.C., where Apostle Kathryn ministered. I came with such hunger and faith that God would release an impartation of anointing to me. My wife and I believe in sowing financially into the Lord's work, so on our way to the National Mall, we also sowed financially into 5F Church.
>
> That day at the mall, Apostle Kathryn declared to the crowd, "From today, you will cast out demons and heal the sick . . . preach the true Gospel with love, compassion and power. That's the Great Commission—to preach the Gospel, heal the sick, cast out demons, and raise the dead. . . . Choose only to love, so He can put this powerful anointing in you, to spread revival through you, and do radical, shocking things through you that will shock the nation, that will make news and that will

transform the whole country and world. Are you willing to rise up and be this change?"

As Apostle Kathryn said this, cries of "Yes!" came from the crowd. I yelled "Yes!" with all my heart. She told us, "God is saying you are called and you are chosen. . . . He is going to release this powerful anointing to you now where you will start to see miracles happen through you. From this day, people will be healed, people will be set free through you because of your heart!"

As she declared this, she lifted her hand and declared, "I release this anointing to you now; be filled now with this anointing. This revival fire that comes with love, and power, I speak miracles to happen through you, healing and deliverance to happen through you, cities to be transformed through you, in Jesus' name!"

The Holy Spirit came upon all of us, and I received by faith with all my heart as I stood there, hands raised to God. I knew I had received! It was one of the most glorious days of my life. The next week when I ministered, I stepped out by faith and acted on the word declared over me. I called people forth, and demons trembled and were cast out as I commanded them to leave in the name of Jesus! God continues to use me in the anointing, with power to preach the Gospel, cast out demons and heal the sick, delivering those who are oppressed by the devil.

The anointing to fulfill the Great Commission has increased not only on my life, but also on my wife's. Lindsey is also an ordained minister, and she also went to the National Mall revival to receive impartation. But she actually experienced multiple deliverances as we traveled to Apostle Kathryn's revival services in different places. She was delivered from generational witchcraft, an orphan spirit, a spirit of infirmity and more! Since a revival service where Apostle Kathryn prophesied an increase of anointing and miracles over her, Lindsey has also been casting out demons and receiving words of knowledge during our own services. Now we both encourage others to do whatever they can to attend revival services like 5F Church's, where God is moving in power and anointing.

## OBED'S IMPARTATION TESTIMONY

Obed Heras grew up in the Christian faith, but did not have a strong role model to teach him how to follow God. Instead of discipling him, some "religious" leaders made him feel condemned and unworthy. He became rebellious and distant from God. More than once, Obed tried to get back on track spiritually, but he didn't know how to break the enemy's yokes and find freedom. He and his wife eventually came to a 5F Church service, however, after seeing a livestream. There, they received deliverance and impartation. Since then, their once-broken lives have never been the same! Here is Obed's testimony:

I felt as if I wasn't good enough to be part of the church, so I rebelled. I was always doing the opposite of what God wanted. I served in music ministry, but I had some really bad influences on me. I would get high on cocaine and play during church services. It was just religion, and I felt so empty inside.

I quit church, but after I got married I wanted to come back to what made me happy, and that was music. My wife and I got involved in some churches, but I went right back to what I used to do, bound by drinking, smoking and sexual immorality for years. I had heard about God being able to heal and free people. Unfortunately, I didn't know how to obtain this freedom. My addictions became stronger. I would go to work and party heavily, without my family knowing. But my children would see a difference when I came home; I could see it in their eyes. Week after week, I would walk out the church doors still bound, with so much guilt and condemnation inside me.

Through it all, I remembered that the Bible talked about healing. One day, I began to get mad about pastors and churches not getting the job done. "Why am I not seeing healings anymore?"

I yelled. "Why am I not seeing miracles?" I told God, "I will do them—just show me HOW!"

From that day, I noticed there was a new spark in me, a new hunger, but I was so demonized that I just couldn't do what God called me to do. One day, my wife sent me a video of Apostle Kathryn. I will never forget that day! I saw a woman being healed in the video. She had crutches, and when Apostle Kathryn prayed, she fell under the anointing. I stopped watching because the demons inside me couldn't handle it. But then I went out to my camper, grabbed some beer as usual, and watched some more. A demon began to manifest in a former worship leader who had been mute for months. I was in shock because I had never seen anything like this. Apostle Kathryn commanded the demon to go out, and the person was set free! Speaking out loud for the first time in many months, this person said, "Thank you, Jesus!" and began singing a worship song.

Right away I said, "I want that!" I told God, *If you're real, God, I want what she just received!* I dumped out all eighteen beers I had bought for the day and said, *I'm sorry, Lord. I repent. Change my life the way you did with that woman!*

At that moment, the spark I had felt before flamed up. I felt so much peace and relief. I told my wife, Cynthia, "We have to make it out to LA to visit 5F Church!" She wanted to go, too, and get set free of depression and anxiety. [You'll read her testimony next.] We had some financial hardship, but God provided. A Jacuzzi had been given to us, and we asked God to help us sell it if He wanted us to visit 5F Church. The Jacuzzi sold, and we used the money to make the trip to LA.

We had our prayers answered at 5F Church! Apostle Kathryn called us to the front and prayed over us. She gave me a powerful word: "Yes, you came to receive freedom, but there's even more for you. God wants to use you in this revival. I see people believing in the real Jesus who comes in power because of you. I see many miracles happening through you."

The power of God touched me so tangibly that I felt as if someone pushed me back. I had never experienced that. Cynthia and I left incredibly happy. I felt overwhelming joy that the flame in me had fully torched into such a hunger and passion for God! I was set free from addiction and so much more that day.

A week later, God started using us in amazing ways. Following His direction, we were able to locate a person thinking about suicide and intervene. When we prayed, that person found freedom and the love of God. I then started seeing the power of God move through me. He used me to deliver family members. Demons trembled in them and left! I work in a sand mine in the oil fields, and I've been praying for my co-workers. I've seen God touch them and deliver them, too!

I am amazed and humbled by how God has used me with His anointing ever since receiving impartation at 5F Church through Apostle Kathryn. A year after we were first delivered, God tugged on my heart, telling me to host a revival in a park, too, where she could come and minister. So many people were set free and touched by God! The word Apostle Kathryn prophesied to me has come to pass. To God my Lord, Jesus Christ, goes all the glory!

## CYNTHIA'S IMPARTATION TESTIMONY

Cynthia Heras, Obed's wife, was raised in a mainline denomination and always believed in God. Yet she never understood how to go beyond religion to having a relationship with Him. She often attended church, but like her husband, she was in bondage to numerous things and did not know how to break free. The same 5F Church service video that she sent her husband (see Obed's testimony) also opened her eyes to God moving in powerful ways she had never experienced, breaking every yoke and setting people free. Cynthia determined that she would find that kind of freedom for herself, and then pass it on to others, as God enabled her. She and her husband visited 5F Church, and both received deliverance and impartation. Here is Cynthia's story:

One night I cried out to God and asked Him to send a man who would love me and my three children. Three months down the road I met my husband, Obed Heras. When we were dating, we visited a small church where God planted a seed in me. The guest speaker talked about preaching in a village going through a drought; God used her to tell the church to go outside because God was bringing rain. And He did, just as she said He would! Her testimony impacted me so much that I said, "I want to hear from God the way she does!"

Afterward, God started growing that seed in me. Obed and I were attending a church in our hometown, and I had given my life to God but hadn't fully surrendered. I was still in bondage, but the conviction in me was so strong that I no longer wanted to continue in my sin. We were still very worldly, however. We were often attacked spiritually through doors we kept opening. Demonic manifestations like hearing growling, feeling a cold evil presence and seeing demons at the end of the bed happened more than once. I was so frightened because I didn't understand what was going on.

God came to my rescue at a time when I needed Him most. Our pastor and some others from church came and prayed over our home, and prayed for me to be baptized in the Holy Spirit, which happened. That same week on Wednesday night, I went to the altar and once again asked God to forgive me and help me change my ways. Someone placed a hand on me, and my body started shaking uncontrollably. I fell to the ground yelling, which was a demonic manifestation. As some people prayed over me, I was set free from so much! The intense fear and postpartum depression took longer, but I stood strong in the Lord, believing His promises and soaking myself in His Word.

After this experience, I began learning more about the spiritual realm. Our church didn't teach much about being equipped, so we began to look for more. We even joined some friends in starting a church, but we were all spiritually immature and it didn't work out. Then Obed and I got involved in another church where they talked about how they used to walk in miracles and see people set free. But we never witnessed any deliverances or healings there. When Covid hit, once again we found ourselves wanting more. We were tired of all the lies and discouragement. We wanted to see the Bible come to life!

Then last year, I came across a video of someone interviewing Apostle Kathryn Krick. The person played a small clip of Apostle Kathryn at "Revival in the Park," casting out demons. It completely blew my mind! This is what Obed and I had been searching for. I texted my husband right away and said, "You need to watch this video *right now*!"

Like me, Obed was shocked and amazed. We decided we would travel to California to experience God's touch. We drove to 5F Church a month after watching Apostle Kathryn on that video. At 5F, I received deliverance from depression, anxiety, fear, suicidal thoughts, not loving my kids the way I wanted to, stagnancy, poverty and much more! My husband received deliverance, too, and also impartation. We've been planted ever since, and I've received more deliverance and anointing.

God placed it in our hearts to bring Apostle Kathryn to New Mexico for revival, and it sure happened! People came from around New Mexico, Texas and even Chihuahua, Mexico, and the move of God was so powerful. Obed and I are walking in God's anointing and can't wait to see what He has in store for us. Now 5F Church is our home church, and we've learned so much in such a short time. We are equipped for spiritual battles. We know how the anointing works with authority, how powerful our words are, how to defeat the devil's lies, how to keep our deliverance, and so much more. God came through for us with healing, deliverance and anointing, and we have been on fire for the Lord ever since we first visited 5F Church.

## GOD IS MORE THAN READY

Out of all these people giving their testimonies of impartation, I only laid hands on a couple of them. You can receive impartation just by planting, sowing and serving. You don't have to have a laying on of hands. You just need to believe that God is releasing the anointing to you. Surrender to God to release His anointing to you in whatever way He wants, whether it's through the laying on of hands, or through being in the crowd at a church or revival service, or even through watching online.

In all these testimonies, from the pastor so desperate for more, to the evangelist longing to see people set free, to the young woman who started a Revival club at school, to the husband and wife who went from being hopelessly bound to being yoke breakers, there are a few consistent factors. These anointed people are humble and childlike, and have a passion to see others set free. They just want to please God, and they don't have selfish ambition. They also consistently watch 5F Church's livestreams or attend in person, so they are continually planting themselves under the flow of anointing. Upon seeing their hearts, I wasn't surprised to see God using them so powerfully.

God is more than ready to release the anointing upon His people, but their hearts have to be pure. God isn't looking at your experience, your credentials, how long you have been a Christian, or if you are a minister and for how long. He isn't looking at if you're male or female, or at your age. God is just looking at your heart. He confounds the wise of this world by the "foolish" people whom He chooses to use.

It's time for those of us in the Body of Christ to transform into true children of God and do what Jesus taught us to do. As He told us, "Truly I tell you, unless you change and become like little children, you will never enter the kingdom of heaven" (Matthew 18:3).

# 9

# Launching Your Calling

His master replied, "Well done, good and faithful servant! You have been faithful with a few things; I will put you in charge of many things. Come and share your master's happiness!"

Matthew 25:23

The anointing is so very precious! God has entrusted you with His great power, and it is so very valuable. God is leading you, but it is up to you how you steward and use that anointing. God gives us a free will, and when you receive the anointing, that truth remains.

That is why there is so much testing and so many spiritual "prerequisites" to receiving the anointing. God needs to really see that He can trust your heart, since He is literally giving true power to you, knowing you have a free will about how you use it. God will lead you every step of the way about how to use it, but you have to decide to obey Him.

I am so glad God has such a thorough process for us to go through before He releases the anointing. Being trusted with the anointing is not something to take lightly. This is a major responsibility. It is a bigger responsibility than being the president of a country. You carry the greatest power in the world. You carry the answer to all the world's problems. You carry the power to save people from committing suicide or dying from cancer. You carry God's power that saves, heals, delivers and does the impossible.

## VALUING GOD'S PROMISES

From day one when I received the prophecy that I was called to carry the anointing, I was so humbled. I could not believe that God would choose me. And to this day, I am still in awe that He did. From day one, I really did not see myself as spiritually advanced or special, someone who had the best prayer life and read enough of the Bible. I felt like such an ordinary person. I am so glad I didn't feel entitled to receive the anointing. That's a dangerous place. What you feel entitled to, you don't value. I felt as though I was being given the most valuable treasure in the world, and I didn't feel worthy of it.

Since day one, I have valued this anointing high above anything else in my life. It would be four and a half years later that I would begin to see many demons cast out and many miracles take place. Yet from day one, I had the revelation that this anointing was truly in me and that I therefore had a great responsibility. I knew the day would come when I would see the prophesied miracles. That day would be the launching of my calling. It would be the beginning of stepping into the fullness of my purpose. I knew the anointing was growing in me all that time, until I would see that day—the promised land of walking in my calling.

I would remind myself daily that I was a vessel of anointing. Being fully surrendered to God and constantly obeying Him became even more important to me. I suppose it's kind of like when a woman becomes pregnant. Taking good care of herself becomes twice as important. I kept reminding myself, *I'm pregnant with this anointing, and I must take care of it. I must make sure this anointing in its fullness (the launching of my calling) is birthed. I must make sure it is birthed in God's perfect timing, not a day late.*

All those complainers among God's people in the wilderness were partly responsible for Moses never seeing the Promised Land, and for others dying in the wilderness and never seeing it, either. Carrying the anointing is weighty! Since March 2021, we have seen thousands be delivered and healed, and God has moved in tremendous power every week at 5F Church and at "Revival Is Now" events in many other places. Thousands all over the world have been watching online and receiving as well. What if I had disobeyed God and lost the anointing? Would some of those people not be delivered today? Would some of the people who were delivered of suicidal spirits have killed themselves? Or what if I had aborted the anointing and given up? Or what if I had rushed things and it had died prematurely?

The Israelites complaining and disobeying on their way to the Promised Land had real consequences. It meant some of them never got there. And today when we don't value the anointing, there can be real consequences. If a chosen, anointed vessel gives up, God can raise up another vessel, but it doesn't happen overnight. Revival could literally be delayed because of disobedience.

Do you see how weighty carrying the anointing is? God convicted me to treasure this anointing and protect it. My church was getting smaller every year, and we only saw miracles once in a while. It looked like the opposite of revival. Yet I reminded myself daily, *I am a vessel of anointing. God's promises will come to pass, and we will see revival now, just as God said.*

I wrote down the promises and prophetic words spoken over me and hung them up on my bedroom wall. I looked at them and meditated on them. I reminded myself that my obedience was leading to seeing these promises fulfilled. I just had to keep obeying. I just had to keep showing up and giving God my best. I just had to keep preaching, editing and posting, and keep on believing.

It's important to write down the promises God has made you and the dreams He has given you. The Lord put it this way to the prophet Habakkuk: "Write the vision and make it plain on tablets, that he may run who reads it" (Habakkuk 2:2 NKJV). There may be times where there is no sign of what God has promised you in the physical realm. Years may pass. But the promise remains! Reminding yourself of the promise helps strengthen your faith and keep the promise alive.

Thank God in advance for the promises He has made you. Many times, I would look at the promises hanging on my wall and pray, *Thank you, God, for the people you will bring to 5F Church who will encounter you and encounter your miraculous power.* Keep your eyes focused on the direction God has given you. Just keep doing what He has told you to do, no matter how "successful" your efforts appear and how much "progress" you've made in the physical realm.

## OBEDIENCE WITH A PURE HEART

What strengthened me the most was knowing that obedience to God is what touches Him the most. It is His love language. God loves all His children. But not all His children touch His heart. You touch God's heart by living your life to please Him and by doing what makes Him happy. With earthly relationships, when you really love someone, what makes you happiest is seeing that person happy. Therefore, you purposefully want to touch that person's heart and bring him or her joy. That's how it is with God. When you really love God, you want to see His heart touched. You want to bring Him joy.

Obedience touches God's heart the most because obeying is the only place where you will be in His will and where you can fulfill your purpose of being His vessel. When you are obeying God and being His vessel, more people can be saved and His Kingdom can advance.

Serving God for the right reasons is what makes the anointing grow healthily in you. You aren't obeying God just so you can reach your dream of walking in the anointing, for your own selfish ambitions. You are obeying God simply because you love Him and want to please Him. Serving with a pure heart protects the anointing in you and makes it grow.

You can't fool God. You may have received prophecies that you are called to be a highly anointed minister. But that will not automatically happen through serving in the Church alone and doing good works. I have seen multiple times when people received a prophecy about being a fivefold minister, or about being called to walk in the anointing, but the anointing was aborted because their hearts weren't pure. There was selfish ambition, and a door for the enemy was left wide open. When the enemy found his chance, he used spirits of jealousy and impatience, and these people stepped out of God's place of receiving the anointing. You need to have a pure heart and serve God with pure intentions to see the anointing stay in you and grow healthily.

## SPEAK UP, AND ONLY SPEAK LIFE

This anointing you carry is to bring the dead to life. The anointing is Jesus, and Jesus is *life*. One entryway for demons opens up when a mother speaks death over the baby in her womb, maybe saying things like "I don't want this baby," or "my life is ruined now." I've seen many people delivered from demons that had entered in the womb. When mothers renounce words of death they have spoken over their child, then the child is delivered. You should only speak life over your children (both in the womb and anytime during their childhood). Otherwise, you are opening the door for demons to come in and steal, kill and destroy your children. Remember, "The tongue has the power of life and death" (Proverbs 18:21).

In the same way, if you speak death over the anointing, your calling and the anointing growing in you could die prematurely. A big part of valuing and protecting the anointing is speaking only life over the anointing in you, and over your life and future. There will be temptations to speak death. Doubting that the promise will come to pass and speaking that doubt aloud is speaking death over the anointing. Words like "I don't know if this prophecy will actually come to pass" speak doubt and death. Speaking death means saying anything that isn't God's will or doesn't align with His truth. Words like "This isn't working" or "I don't know if I'm good enough or if I have what it takes" actually speak death over yourself and your future.

As I told you, for more than four years there was pretty much no sign that we were even getting closer to the "promised land" of revival. In fact, 5F Church was actually getting smaller and the views online weren't growing. But I never spoke words like "This isn't working" or "I don't know if those prophecies were true or will ever come to pass." For all those years, I made a promise to God that I would only speak life over my future and I would always come into agreement with the promises He had made me. I never wanted to do anything that would make me lose the anointing, so I became so careful only to speak life, and to speak and act in faith every single day.

I spoke *Revival Is Now* enthusiastically for three and a half years just about every single week, with only between one and twenty people in the congregation. In the middle of that time, I wrote a song with Jeanntal called "Revival Is Now" and sang it regularly at church, prophesying that revival is truly now and that we were about to see signs, wonders and miracles any day.

I would feel so discouraged and sad when people would leave our ministry. But I would not voice anything but faith. I would speak words like these:

"I trust God."

"We must be going higher!"

"This is another test where God is refining me so I can receive more anointing."

"This is the cost of the anointing."

"I can't wait for the promises to come to pass!"

Though I was not seeing tons of physical evidence that the anointing was in me, the way I do daily today, I kept reminding myself, *I am carrying powerful anointing that can really bring change right now*. Though there is a time when the launching of your calling and stepping into the promised land takes place, that doesn't mean the anointing isn't flowing through you until then. The moment you start receiving anointing, God wants to use you. I knew God was trusting me to steward the anointing properly from day one. I carried the revelation *This anointing is in me!*

When I would preach to just a small number of people, I would remind myself, *The anointing is in me, and God is going to touch these people powerfully today*. When I would interact with people in daily life, like the person doing my nails or cutting my hair, I would carry the revelation *God wants to touch this person through me!* When I would share my testimony, talk to people about God or pray for them, I would remember that I carried the anointing and that they were going to experience the power of God. I knew God was asking me to renew my mind with the truth of the anointing being in me, so that the anointing could grow, and so that I could grow spiritually.

When you carry the anointing, you carry real power. When you speak words of life (God's will) as His vessel, those prayers and prophecies carry much greater power than before you received the anointing. Because of that, you have to be careful not to curse your life or other people with your words. If you haphazardly speak words of death, they also carry greater power. You must have the fear of God when you carry the anointing and always remember the true power you carry. When you are going through the wilderness season, God will test how you use this power. God releases the anointing in stages so that you don't misuse the anointing and cause major damage. He takes you step by step to teach you how to use the anointing carefully and completely within His will.

## BEING INTENTIONAL WITH THE ANOINTING

When I first received the anointing, I became more careful and intentional than ever always to speak God's will over myself and other people. I made sure to love people the very best I could. I made sure not to withhold the anointing, but always to release it through prayers and prophetic words, whenever God led me to. I would give my all for every sermon. It was out of my comfort zone to pray for people one-on-one in the beginning, but I reminded myself, *The people need this anointing! I must be obedient to release what God has given me.*

I would call people forward to pray for them. So many times, I would feel uncomfortable because I didn't know what to say. But every time I started praying for people, God would give me the words to say, and they would be prophetic words someone needed to hear. So often, I would see people cry as I started praying for them. Even when certain people did mean things to me, I would be so careful only to speak life and love over them, reminding myself, *This anointing is precious, and I don't want to do anything to misuse or abuse it.*

"If you are faithful in little things, you will be faithful in large ones. But if you are dishonest in little things, you won't be honest with greater responsibilities" (Luke 16:10 NLT). I felt a strong conviction from God that I must be faithful with what He entrusted me. I reminded myself many times that it is such an honor to be entrusted with even ten people to lead and pastor. God didn't have to trust me with them, but He did, and I had to value that. I humbled myself and was careful not to complain that there weren't more people and that the promises weren't coming to pass fast enough.

In those years before the first demon was cast out, many times I would declare darkness to go as I prayed for people. I would look at people with love, putting all my focus on them. *God, what is your heart for them?* is how I would speak in my heart. I would give my all to be a pure vessel of God for that person in that moment. Sometimes, for example, I would declare that depression, anxiety and suicidal thoughts must leave a person. There would not be manifestations, though sometimes there were tears. You couldn't see demons leaving, but I was doing what God had called me to do—destroying the works of the devil in people's lives and declaring God's will and heart over them.

It's not as if I hadn't been praying for people at all, and then one day I did and demons just started being cast out. For years, I had been continually declaring over people that darkness must flee and that God's will would be done. God was testing me: Did I really know what this anointing was for? Would I use it properly by faithfully praying for people and praying the right way? Would I be confident, knowing that He was moving and things were happening in the spiritual realm as I spoke, even if I didn't see anything yet? When the first demon was cast out, I was doing what I had been doing for years every single Sunday—declaring that darkness must go and allowing God to speak through me as I prayed for someone. So be encouraged if you are in the place that I was—believing God to use you in the anointing, but not seeing "results" yet. Step out in faith and obedience! You have to start somewhere to be entrusted with more. The important thing when you have been entrusted with the anointing is to start doing what God has called you to do. Jesus tells this parable about the Kingdom of heaven:

> It will be like a man going on a journey, who called his servants and entrusted his wealth to them. To one he gave five bags of gold, to another two bags, and to another one bag, each according to his ability. Then he went on his journey.
>
> Matthew 25:14–15

Here's what happened when the man returned home:

> After a long time the master of those servants returned and settled accounts with them. The man who had received five bags of gold brought the other five. "Master," he said, "you entrusted me with five bags of gold. See, I have gained five more."
>
> His master replied, "Well done, good and faithful servant! You have been faithful with a few things; I will put you in charge of many things. Come and share your master's happiness!"
>
> Verses 19–21

The servant with two bags of gold did the same:

> "Master," he said, "you entrusted me with two bags of gold; see, I have gained two more."
>
> His master replied, "Well done, good and faithful servant! You have been faithful with a few things; I will put you in charge of many things. Come and share your master's happiness!"
>
> Verses 22–23

But the servant with the one bag didn't put any effort into growing what the master had entrusted him with:

Then the man who had received one bag of gold came. "Master," he said, "I knew that you are a hard man, harvesting where you have not sown and gathering where you have not scattered seed. So I was afraid and went out and hid your gold in the ground. See, here is what belongs to you."

His master replied, "You wicked, lazy servant! So you knew that I harvest where I have not sown and gather where I have not scattered seed? Well then, you should have put my money on deposit with the bankers, so that when I returned I would have received it back with interest.

"So take the bag of gold from him and give it to the one who has ten bags. For whoever has will be given more, and they will have an abundance. Whoever does not have, even what they have will be taken from them."

Verses 24–29

The master took the bag of gold from the servant who had done nothing with it and gave it to the responsible, faithful servant who had started with five bags and had multiplied those to ten. Just as we see in this parable, at first God will give you a "small" amount of anointing, and then He will watch to see what you do with it. Don't despise the small beginnings, because you have to start small in order for God to see that you can be entrusted with more.

Also, God is giving you the anointing not for yourself, but to minister to others. If you keep the anointing to yourself, you are like the servant with one bag of gold who buried it to hide it. The servants with five bags and two bags went out and produced many more because they stewarded what they had been entrusted with well. You are like those faithful servants when you use the anointing in every moment God is leading you to. Every time people are in need of prayer, don't hold back. Speak life over them, whether that is declaring darkness must go, or declaring healing or a prophetic word of encouragement.

When people in your life feel down, don't be quiet. Encourage them, and give them hope.

Remind yourself that even if you are not hearing tons of testimonies about miracles God has done through your prayers, the anointing really is in you and God is using you to touch people's lives by His power and love. Every time you pray for someone or preach or teach (whether it's to a large congregation or to just one person), remind yourself, *God's power is moving through me now and touching these people. I will not withhold, but will pour out all God has entrusted to me.* "Freely you have received; freely give" (Matthew 10:8).

### GET TO WORK!

When you have received the anointing, get to work! Don't sit by and wait for the promised land to come. Don't sit by and wait for miracles to just suddenly burst out of you. You need to use, steward and protect that anointing. Follow the Holy Spirit's leading in how He wants you to release it. Use your gifts to serve and help advance His Kingdom. Use the anointing to minister to your co-workers, family and friends, and whomever God brings to you. The purpose of the anointing is to serve others. You have it to bless others. You have it to release healing and deliverance to others. You have it to open people's eyes to God's love and to release His truth. So you must be releasing the anointing to others.

One of the biggest ways God wants you to release the anointing is to share your testimony: "For the testimony of Jesus is the spirit of prophecy" (Revelation 19:10 NKJV). Sharing your testimony of how the anointing of Jesus set you free, healed you, opened your eyes and was imparted to you to walk in God's power releases faith to others so they can receive, too. I can't tell you how many times I have shared my testimony of what this anointing has done for my life and how God has used the anointing in me to touch others. In the beginning, it was all I had.

Sharing your testimony is being faithful with what God has given you. You may not think you have a lot to share with others, but your testimony is more than enough! Your testimony carries the power to change someone's life. Your testimony carries the power to release faith for others to be able to receive miracles. I always felt such conviction to share my testimony in its entirety, with all truth. Many people I have shared with didn't know about anointing, impartation, deliverance and other such spiritual truths that are vital to understand. As the Bible says, "My people are destroyed for lack of knowledge" (Hosea 4:6 KJV). Yet it also says, "And you will know the truth, and the truth will set you free" (John 8:32 NLT).

Don't be shy and withhold your testimony of how Jesus through His anointing has changed your life. Release your testimony the best you can, and as much as you can, as often as you can. This is how, from day one of receiving it, the anointing will be released so powerfully in your life. This is how you pass the test that proves you value this anointing and will steward it well, so God can increase it in you.

## VALUE ENCOURAGEMENT FROM GOD

God encouraged me through another person's powerful testimony, which strengthened my faith in the anointing He placed in me. Jeanntal came to 5F Church nine months after I started the church. She has been at church almost every Sunday since then, and she is now such an important part of carrying out the work of God both at 5F Church and at the "Revival Is Now" events I minister at around the world. This is Jeanntal's testimony:

> Before I came to 5F Church in 2018, I felt as if I had been wandering lost in a desert. I got baptized with the Holy Spirit

at seventeen, and I just wanted to run and tell everyone about Jesus! He lit me on fire, but boys and relationships then became a huge distraction. I lived a lukewarm Christian life for years. There had been a huge falling away in my old church, so the community I had been part of was gone and I was left with so much "church hurt." For five years, I bounced from church to church, or for weeks on end I wouldn't even bother to go. But one day in April 2018, my mom told me about this small church in Hollywood. "You should check it out," she said. "They pray for everyone at the end of the service."

I shrugged my shoulders and said, "Sure, why not." At that moment, I had no idea that this small yes would be the second-best decision of my life!

My first day at 5F Church was when the services were being held in the basement of the Hollywood Legion, where you had to go through a kitchen just to get to the room. I'll never forget the first face that greeted me. It was Apostle Kathryn's, and she welcomed me with such kindness and love that it forever left a mark on my heart. Sometimes I think of God rejoicing when that moment happened. I had no idea that I had just met the person who would become my spiritual mom, apostle, and the greatest friend of my life.

I fell in love with 5F Church from the start. I soon noticed that as I went week after week, I was changing. I was falling deeper in love with Jesus, and the teachings were feeding my spirit. I was growing; I was learning! For the first time in my life, temptations and issues I had struggled with for years were just falling away, without strife. The anointing was transforming me with zero effort of my own. It was all Jesus! The past Jeanntal is now gone. Who was that woman? Jesus' anointing has forever changed me. It has matured me and created a new person who is fully surrendered and full of joy!

My heart burns for others to receive this anointing, because I know what it can do. It has now become one of my greatest passions to see people be planted where the anointing is. If you can just stay still where God's power is moving, if you serve and don't move an inch, you will see God do wonders in your life. Stay, serve and receive! Jeremiah 17:8 says "They will be like a tree planted by the water that sends out its roots by the stream. It does not fear when heat comes; its leaves are always green. It has no worries in a year of drought and never fails to bear fruit." I want you to receive what I have!

Apostle Kathryn's pure, beautiful heart has been my greatest teacher. I've learned so much not only through her anointed, meaty teachings, but through witnessing her dedication and surrender to Jesus. I've watched her work so hard for the Kingdom—editing late into the nights, getting equipment set up for our fifteen or fewer attendees so 5F Church would represent Christ with excellence. She never stopped working hard, even when people would leave the church. Her steadfastness has taught me so much.

When you find a rare gem, you hold on to it and cherish it. I found a rare gem in 5F Church. When you encounter a church where the anointing is flowing, do whatever you need to do so that you never let the enemy pull you away. Hold on to the precious gift God has given you! I couldn't be more grateful to Jesus for radically changing my life. His wonderful kindness brought me to 5F Church and allowed me to taste and see His goodness. *Jesus, you are simply everything to me!*

Jeanntal's testimony strengthened and encouraged me so much. It helped me see that the anointing truly is in me, even though initially I didn't see tons of evidence. She was a huge, beautiful fruit of my ministry, and it encouraged me so much. Looking at her, I knew that one day there would be many more lives transformed by the anointing. If God could do it for Jeanntal, He would do it for many others!

In the wilderness seasons when the promised land may seem far away, God will give you signs that you are on the right track and that the anointing really is in you. Treasure those signs! They will strengthen you to keep going and keep pouring out the anointing with everything in you.

As you are reading this book, you may be in a season of carrying the anointing but having yet to reach your promised land. Look for the signs God has given you along the way, the encouragement that His power is truly moving through you and that you are making amazing progress. Someday your consistent obedience and your stewardship of the anointing is going to result in promises fulfilled and great reward!

God has such tremendous plans to use you mightily. May your awareness in the spiritual realm increase to see what you are carrying, and may you carry the fear of God to obey Him step by step and speak your every word with care and intention. Take a moment today to write down and meditate on the promises God has made you. And thank Him in advance for these precious promises coming to pass in your life!

# 10

# Releasing the Anointing Effectively

This dear woman, a daughter of Abraham, has been held in bondage by Satan for eighteen years. Isn't it right that she be released, even on the Sabbath?

Luke 13:16 NLT

Everyone has different callings and different giftings. Also, there will be different seasons where God uses you in unique ways. You must follow the leading of the Holy Spirit about how exactly He wants to use you.

Before the first demon was cast out, the Holy Spirit led me to pray for individuals and allow the prophetic anointing to flow through me. I would call out a person in the congregation, and God would fill my mouth with words to pray for him or her. This was a big leap of faith for me, but God was faithful every time, giving me words that truly were exactly what He needed that person to hear. Many times, the person's response would be tears and a look of awe, like, *Wow, God really hears my prayers. God really knows me, and He's with me!* Sometimes

God would lead me to lay a hand on someone. Sometimes He would lead me just to put my hand out and declare, "I release this anointing." Sometimes He would lead me to pray for people to receive the baptism of the Holy Spirit.

And then on the day I told you about in chapter 3, March 21, 2021, I was ministering in the way the Holy Spirit had been leading me for a few years. I called this woman forward, and God filled my mouth with prophetic prayers for her. I said, "Those attacks against you keeping you from receiving from God—I declare them to be broken off you! I see the fire of God coming upon you now," and she fell back with the power of God.

A demon then convulsed in her, which was the first time I had seen that happen in my ministry. The Holy Spirit led me to minister in a way I never had before. I spoke with boldness and authority, fearless of the demon. I commanded it to go, and it left. From that day, God shifted how He was using me for this new season. Within two months, hundreds poured into our park services to encounter the anointing and be set free. Now, I minister all around the world, as well as at 5F Church, usually a total of three to five times per week. I specifically minister to many who need deliverance and healing, and I also release impartation. God has led many people bound by demons to come to 5F Church, or to the "Revival Is Now" services across the world, to encounter the anointing that will heal them and set them free.

This great shift in the way God was using me started out mostly with me prophetically encouraging and edifying people, and teaching the Word of God. Then it went to me preaching the Gospel, healing the sick, casting out demons, praying for people to receive the baptism of the Holy Spirit and releasing impartation, but with a huge emphasis on casting out demons. God was leading people to come receive freedom at my services, so He needed me to cast out demons.

I had to adapt and move with the Holy Spirit. I never really craved casting out demons, but God wanted to use me mightily to cast them out. I happily adapted and followed the Holy Spirit. I can't get tired of casting out demons, because there is nothing more beautiful in the world than seeing the look on people's faces once Jesus sets them free, and once they have this revelation that Jesus loves them so much that He has rescued them and delivered them from their torturous bondage.

## FOLLOWING THE HOLY SPIRIT

I have to really listen to the Holy Spirit as I minister. I might desire to cast out demons from someone and then take the time to prophesy to that person for a while. But I must obey God when He is instead saying, *This is an emergency! My children are in bondage—hundreds of them, and right now I have sent you on a mission to deliver them, not to prophesy at length. This is your assignment for right now!* I have to follow the Holy Spirit's lead in that moment and shift gears to accomplish whatever is on God's heart to get done.

In this season, the way God leads me to minister looks so different from what I ever imagined it would. It looks entirely different from how I ministered a little over a year ago. And there will be different seasons ahead. For example, right now God is reviving the deliverance ministry. It was almost completely absent from the Body of Christ for so long, and now it is being revived all over the world. This means there are so many people who need freedom! Once the revival spreads more and more, and once more people have been delivered, we won't be in so much of an *Emergency! Everyone needs deliverance!* mode. At that point, the Holy Spirit will be leading in new ways.

So when there comes this "launching your calling" season where the anointing is pouring out of you like never before, it is important to be very sensitive to how the Holy Spirit is leading you. Give all control to Him, and let Him take the reins. God may ask you to move in a new way. Don't listen to naysayers who don't understand you and weren't called to be the voice of God in your life. Only follow His voice.

The first demon I cast out left with a simple command and without my laying a hand on the woman. This is how God wanted to use me to show the great power of the anointing, and to demonstrate that we don't need to get in the way with our human efforts and loud voice in order for God to work. He wanted to use me in simplicity to show that He is the one who does every miracle, and that He doesn't need our help. We are just simple vessels, but it is His mighty power that does every miracle.

The way in which God was using me—with a simple command, not loudly, and without touching the person—was unique. Some had not seen deliverance done in that "style" before. But remember that God led the apostle Peter to demonstrate the powerful authority the anointing carries just by having his shadow fall on people. The sick and demon possessed were healed and delivered without Peter shouting at demons or touching people. This was a new "style" of deliverance that Scripture doesn't record Jesus doing.

God likewise led the apostle Paul to demonstrate the great power and simplicity of the anointing by leading him to touch handkerchiefs. Then when those handkerchiefs were placed on the sick or demon possessed, these people would be healed and delivered. This was also a new deliverance "style" that we don't see Jesus doing in the Bible.

God always moves in new, unexpected ways. "I will destroy the wisdom of the wise," He said, "and the understanding of those who have understanding, I will confound" (1 Corinthians 1:19 NASB). God moves outside the box and in ways we aren't expecting. We cannot limit how He wants to move.

When God begins to use you in power, you will definitely find yourself becoming the target of criticism from people with the religious spirit, just as what happened to Jesus. The devil hates the anointing because it is the power that destroys his works. The way he attacks the anointing is by sending the religious spirit to people, who then attack the anointing in others. They call something "not of God" just because they have never seen God move that particular way. The devil whispers lies that what they are seeing is demonic power, just as the Pharisees accused Jesus of using Beelzebul's power to cast out demons. But Jesus ministered with a revelation the Pharisees didn't have. One time, He healed a woman on the Sabbath. According to the Law, one couldn't do any kind of work on the Sabbath. The Pharisees considered healing the woman as work, so they accused Jesus of breaking the Law.

But Jesus was coming in a new way, with new revelation. He told the Pharisees, "This dear woman, a daughter of Abraham, has been held in bondage by Satan for eighteen years. Isn't it right that she be released, even on the Sabbath?" (Luke 13:16 NLT). God was manifested through Jesus so mightily through the love, compassion and miracles! But the Pharisees missed God completely. Their closed minds and pride did not allow them to see that the God they worshiped was just coming through Jesus in a new way they hadn't seen before! Jesus was following the leading of the Father, but the Pharisees thought the opposite.

From the first time a demon was cast out in my ministry, God has used me in a unique way. The way demons were cast out looked different than what most were used to seeing. Yet there was so much support and excitement in the beginning. It seemed as though everyone was happily accepting the new way God was moving. But then the devil began to get extremely angry. You could see a shift in the spiritual realm where all of a sudden, attacks came against me. Most had to do with people being uncomfortable that God was using me differently. Instead of seeing the beauty in what God was doing, some people would criticize and say, "That's not how you cast out demons!" Others would say, "There are no more apostles today!" And still others would say, "Women cannot be pastors or apostles!" Most had never seen a female apostle who was also casting out demons.

God would give me revelation, releasing prophetic keys about how a person with deep torment could be delivered. For example, one woman brought her young son to a "Revival is Now" event in another city, where I was ministering. She traveled from afar, desperate for her young son to be delivered. She had brought him to many ministers, and the demons in him would manifest, but he wouldn't be set free. When she saw my videos, she had hope that he would be delivered.

As I began praying for this woman's son, God revealed to me prophetically that his mom had given a lot of money in the demonic realm. I asked her about it, and she said that over the years she had given several hundred dollars to a psychic. The Bible says what you sow, you will reap. She had reaped bondage for her son. What would cancel that reaping and set her son free? Sowing into the Kingdom of God, where God's anointing is! I told her the key was to sow wherever God's anointing is. It was not about sowing into 5F Church, of course! She could sow anywhere the power of God was moving. It's a spiritual act that has nothing to do with a certain ministry receiving money. Instead, it's a spiritual act of sowing and reaping the anointing of God to cancel that bondage.

I related this prophetic word to her, and then I began to minister to others. About five minutes later, she came over to me with her son. She says, "I took my phone out and sowed online into 5F Church. A few seconds later, my son starts coughing stuff up, and now he's set free!"

I looked at him and he was totally free, smiling so big. The next night, which was day two of "Revival is Now" in that city, she testified and brought her son up with her.* He was completely free and full of joy!

The idea of sowing into the Kingdom to cancel what she and her son were reaping from the enemy was a prophetic key God released specifically for this woman's situation, because of the way the enemy had bound her son in chains. However, this might not be the case for everyone, depending on the situation and revelation. She also didn't "pay for deliverance," as some detractors claimed. Rather, she was doing a spiritual act of sowing into the Kingdom of God, where she then reaped freedom from the deficit of sowing into the devil's kingdom, and reaped freedom for her son!

"Do not be deceived: God is not mocked, for whatever one sows, that will he also reap" (Galatians 6:7 ESV). There is power in making sacrifices to God. Throughout Scripture, we see the miraculous hand of God moving after someone makes a sacrifice or offering to Him:

—*God held back a plague after David sacrificed offerings to Him.*
So David purchased the threshing floor and the oxen for fifty shekels of silver. David built an altar to the LORD there, and offered burnt offerings and peace offerings. So the LORD was moved [to compassion] by [David's] prayer for the land, and the plague was held back from Israel.

2 Samuel 24:24–25 AMP

—*God decided never to destroy humanity again after Noah sacrificed offerings to Him.*
And Noah built an altar to the LORD, and took of every [ceremonially] clean animal and of every clean bird and offered burnt offerings on the altar. The LORD smelled the pleasing

*You can watch her whole testimony at www.youtube.com/watch?v=Xq0b YGvKwXs.

aroma [a soothing, satisfying scent] and the LORD said to Himself, "I will never again curse the ground because of man, for the intent (strong inclination, desire) of man's heart is wicked from his youth; and I will never again destroy every living thing, as I have done."

Genesis 8:20–21 AMP

*—God told Solomon He would give him whatever he asked after Solomon sacrificed offerings to Him.*
The king went to Gibeon [near Jerusalem, where the tabernacle and the bronze altar stood] to sacrifice there, for that was the great high place. Solomon offered a thousand burnt offerings on that altar. In Gibeon the LORD appeared to Solomon in a dream at night; and God said, "Ask [Me] what I shall give you."

1 Kings 3:4–5 AMP

Some cases of demonic oppression are more complex than others. In the section just ahead, "Deliverance—How to Do It," we'll look more closely at how to do deliverance in various cases. But briefly, some deliverance only requires a couple of keys: (1) a person coming to Jesus with faith, believing He can deliver him or her, and (2) encountering an anointed vessel who is praying with authority to release the anointing that destroys the yoke. In other instances, another key may be needed to unlock the chains: (3) specifically renouncing areas of bondage—past open doors to the devil, and demonic covenants. This might also include throwing away objects that have demonic attachments (like crystals, evil-eye jewelry, occult books, Ouija boards, etc.). Finally, for some cases an additional prophetic key might even be revealed, especially when a person or family's past generations have been deeply involved with witchcraft (for example, sowing heavily into the demonic kingdom, as the mother I just told you about had done).

God says, "See, I am doing a new thing" (Isaiah 43:19). He also says that you and I will do greater things than He did! That means the Holy Spirit will release new revelations that haven't been written or recorded yet in the Word. These will always align with the Word of God and with God's principles, of course, and with His will to destroy the devil's works and free His people. "But to each one is given the manifestation of the Spirit [the spiritual illumination and the enabling of the Holy Spirit] for the common good" (1 Corinthians 12:7 AMP; see also verses 4–7). Jesus spit in the dirt to make it into mud and then spread the mud on a blind man's eyes. When the man washed away the mud, he could see! This healing came in a new way never before recorded. People who had known this man when he was blind brought him to the Pharisees and told them about his miraculous healing. The Pharisees immediately denounced Jesus because the miracle had happened on the Sabbath. They couldn't see the beautiful fruit of the man being healed. They could only see that in their opinion, Jesus was going against the Word of God. They could only say, "This man is not from God, for he does not keep the Sabbath" (John 9:16). Jesus was still observing the Sabbath, but He was coming with a new revelation that the Pharisees could not understand out of self-righteousness and pride.

The video of the deliverance of the little boy whose mother had sown into the devil's kingdom was seen by many online, and several people came against the act of the mother sowing a seed. They completely missed the beauty of the child being set free, and instead were saying it was not of God! It reminded me so much of how when Jesus delivered and healed people, all the religious leaders could see was that He "broke the Law" by healing on the Sabbath. Jesus was moving in a new way, with new revelation, and people were being delivered and healed like no one had ever seen! Yet the Pharisees missed it and even accused Him of using demonic powers to cast out demons.

When such religious attacks came against me, it was a new testing I had to go through. The question was, *Did I fear God, or only fear people?* Many wanted me to stick to doing deliverance in a certain "style," without releasing prophetic keys such as the key I released to the mother of this young boy. I felt pressure to conform to how people wanted me to minister, yet I knew that if I listened to them, I would be disobeying God. God has entrusted me to follow His voice and do exactly as He says to see people delivered. If I don't listen to His voice, fewer people, or maybe none, would be delivered in my ministry. So there was this testing: *Will you neglect the people who need freedom if their freedom requires a prophetic key that will offend the religious?*

I chose to obey God over mankind. God commanded King Saul to kill all the enemies and livestock in a battle with the Amalekites (see 1 Samuel 15). But Saul and the people with him wanted to leave some of the animals alive to sacrifice. Saul feared the people over God and disobeyed His command. Because of that, God stripped him of the anointing. To fear people over God comes with serious consequences.

You have to understand that the religious spirit is as active today as it was in Jesus' time. If you're walking in the anointing, the religious spirit will attack. Be prepared for those attacks. Stay faithful to God, and don't give an ear to the critics. God will direct you about how He wants you to use and release His anointing. Only follow His voice. Surrender to Him, and allow Him to use you in exactly the way He desires. Although there may be many "Pharisees" against you, there will be more for you. Remember what the prophet Elisha told his servant: "Don't be afraid. . . . Those who are with us are more than those who are with them" (2 Kings 6:16). There will be more people who see that God is with you and who are grateful for the anointing you carry that blesses them. God will scatter your enemies. Stay strong when the attacks come. They are only temporary. False accusations can never stand. God will reveal that He is with you. The truth always prevails!

## DELIVERANCE—HOW TO DO IT

There are so many people who need freedom. God is trusting you to be prepared to pray for those who need deliverance, whenever He needs you to. And when it's time for the anointing to be released through you to deliver the oppressed, God will bring people to you who need deliverance.

> And these signs shall follow them that believe; In my name shall they cast out devils; they shall speak with new tongues; they shall take up serpents; and if they drink any deadly thing, it shall not hurt them; they shall lay hands on the sick, and they shall recover.
>
> Mark 16:17–18 KJV

How do you use the anointing to set people free? As we have seen, there are certain keys that unlock a person's freedom. Most of the time, deliverance requires these two keys, and sometimes it requires the third:

1. A person coming to Jesus with faith, believing He can deliver.
2. An anointed vessel praying with authority to release the anointing that destroys the yoke.
3. A person renouncing areas of bondage—past open doors to the devil, and demonic covenants.

It's important that you understand this and follow the Holy Spirit's lead. It's always vital that a person come with faith in Jesus for deliverance, and that an anointed vessel is praying with authority for him or her. And then often (but not always), it's necessary for the person to renounce past open doors and demonic covenants. Otherwise, you could be saying "Demons, go!" and they don't leave because the person hasn't done his or her part in unlocking the deliverance. (On occasion, there may also be a prophetic key that's needed, as in the example I gave you of the mother who sowed into God's Kingdom to cancel the bondage that resulted from her sowing into the demonic kingdom in the past.)

### 1. A person coming to Jesus with faith, believing He can deliver.

The Bible tells us about a woman who had a bleeding disorder for twelve years:

> When she heard about Jesus, she came up behind him in the crowd and touched his cloak, because she thought, "If I just touch his clothes, I will be healed." Immediately her bleeding stopped and she felt in her body that she was freed from her suffering.
>
> Mark 5:27–29

When Jesus found out who had touched Him, He said to her, "Daughter, your faith has healed you. Go in peace and be freed from your suffering" (verse 34). Immediately after that, He told Jarius, a synagogue leader whose daughter had just died, "Don't be afraid; just believe" (verse 36). Then Jarius's daughter woke up, and she was healed. In both miracles, faith was the key. Today, faith is still a key that unlocks the miracle. This is why Jesus instructed Jarius to "believe" so that the miracle could take place. In Jesus' hometown He could do hardly any miracles, however, and the reason was because of people's unbelief (see Matthew 13:57–58).

We also see that as the apostles in the Acts Church ministered, faith was still a key that unlocked healing and deliverance:

> In Lystra there sat a man who was lame. He had been that way from birth and had never walked. He listened to Paul as he was speaking. Paul looked directly at him, saw that he had faith to be healed and called out, "Stand up on your feet!" At that, the man jumped up and began to walk.
>
> Acts 14:8–10

Because the lame man had faith, the miracle could take place. Looking at him, Paul saw that the man "had faith to be healed," so Paul declared, "Stand up on your feet!"

In Hosea 4:6 God says, "My people are destroyed from lack of knowledge." Many people perish and do not receive healing and deliverance because of their lack of knowledge about what Jesus provided for them on the cross. "By His stripes we are healed" (Isaiah 53:5 NKJV). Jesus endured scourging, which made stripes on His back. The blood He was shedding as He endured that scourging literally was purchasing your healing today!

Romans 8:16–17 (NLT) says, "For his Spirit joins with our spirit to affirm that we are God's children. And since we are his children, we are his heirs." When you give your life to Jesus, you become a child of God, with a true inheritance. That inheritance is abundant life, as Jesus told us: "The thief comes only to steal and kill and destroy; I have come that they may have life, and have it to the full" (John 10:10). Jesus died on the cross not only to remove all your sins, tear the veil so you can have relationship with God and live eternally in heaven, but *also* so you can have abundant life (life to the full) here on this earth. He died so you can be healed and delivered from the works of the devil here and now. Healing and freedom are your inheritance. They are your right as a child of God.

The woman with the issue of blood thought, *If only I touch the hem of Jesus' garment* . . . She *knew* Jesus wanted to heal her and *would* heal her if she came to Him. The kind of faith that releases miracles is faith that understands this spiritual truth—that healing and freedom *are* God's will for you, that God *can* do it, and that He *will* do it. This kind of faith understands that Jesus already purchased your healing and freedom; you just need to receive it now! You need to accept and claim your inheritance.

When you encounter someone in need of healing or freedom, it's important that you share the full Gospel with them, including this part that they might not have heard before. Many believers are unaware of this truth about coming in faith to receive everything Jesus purchased for them with His blood. Share with people the meaning of "by His stripes you are healed," and share that healing and deliverance truly belong to them as their inheritance. People need to know this so they can have faith to be set free. "Then you will know the truth, and the truth will set you free" (John 8:32).

### 2. An anointed vessel praying with authority to release the anointing that destroys the yoke

It is the anointing that destroys the yoke. When God leads a person in bondage to come to you for freedom, it's time for you as an anointed vessel to execute the authority of Christ you possess and release the anointing to break the chains. Execute your authority over the demons by commanding them. You can often use a simple command such as, "I command every spirit to leave now." If a person shares with you something specific, however—for example that he or she suffers from anxiety—command specifically, "Spirit of anxiety, you must go." Or the Holy Spirit may lead you prophetically to command a specific spirit to go. There is no formula; follow the leading of the Holy Spirit.

Sometimes, the Holy Spirit may lead you to ask a person if he or she would like to renounce anything (refer to key 3 just ahead, where I talk about this in more detail). After a person has renounced specific bondages, use your God-given authority to release the anointing that destroys the yoke. You can say, for example, "I detach you from what you have renounced, and I command that every demonic spirit attached to you must leave you now." In some cases; the bondage might be deeper and more complex and need more keys to unlock every chain. Demonic covenants are one example of what can bring deeper torment. If a person has said "I want to die" or has made a pact with the devil with words like "I'll give up my happiness if you save my relative," this results in deeper bondage. Many times, it's vital for a person to renounce these specific covenants (the specific words that were spoken).

### 3. Renouncing areas of bondage—past open doors and demonic covenants

Many times, a key needed to unlock deliverance is *renouncing*. Renouncing means to abandon something that you once claimed. God has given you authority to either choose the devil's will or His will. When you choose God's will, you are opening the door in the spiritual realm for God's blessings and the inheritance of abundant life to come upon your life. At the same time, you are shutting the door to demons.

On the flip side, when you say yes to the devil's will, you are literally blocking God's blessings from your life, and you are giving the devil authority over your life. This is how doors are opened for demons to come in, and how they enter a person. Here are some examples of saying yes to the devil's will:

—Disobeying God's Word by engaging in witchcraft (e.g., going to psychics, using tarot cards, playing with Ouija

boards, believing in horoscopes, believing in crystals
for healing, using sage in your house for the purpose of
"protecting the home," etc.)

—Getting drunk or using other substances that abuse the
temple (body) God gave you and quench the Holy Spirit

—Having sex with people outside marriage, watching
porn, or engaging in other illicit sexual activities

—Watching demonic movies, listening to demonic music
(music with dark themes such as sexual immorality or
death)

—Speaking death over yourself with words like these: *I
hate myself. This sickness/pain won't go away, and I
think I might die from it. I don't like myself. I'm stupid.
I'll always be poor. I don't think my dreams will ever
come true.*

—Making demonic covenants (i.e., making deals with the
devil or pacts with cults; saying you want to die, etc.)

Sometimes you didn't say yes to the devil's will yourself, but
your parents or grandparents opened a door to demons by saying yes to his will. This is how generational curses occur. When
your ancestors engaged in witchcraft or served the enemy in
some way, doors can be opened for demons to come into your
life. Also, when abuse happens to you, another door can be
opened for demons to come in.

To *renounce* areas of bondage means to use the authority
God has given you. Use the power of life that's in your tongue,
in your words, to renounce the devil's hold on your life and
to say yes only to God's will. As we saw in Proverbs 18:21
earlier, "Death and life are in the power of the tongue, and
those who love it will eat its fruits" (ESV). There is such power
in your tongue when you speak! When you are in bondage and
a key that unlocks you is renouncing, it's as though there are

chains around you and each chain represents a demon. When you renounce things—for example, "I renounce addiction" or "I renounce anxiety"—it is as though the lock on the chain of addiction or on the chain of anxiety has been unlocked, and now the anointing can destroy that heavy chain that was wrapped around you.

If people who need freedom come and ask you to pray for them, explain what renouncing is. Then ask them what they would like to renounce. Encourage them to renounce specific things. Many times, the key is to renounce bondages specifically. "I renounce all sin" is usually not a key that unlocks that lock of bondage. The key is in speaking out specific things like "I renounce depression." If a person has spoken the words "I want to die," technically in the spiritual realm he or she has made a covenant with a demon of suicide/death. Many times, in this case "I renounce suicide" is not enough. A person needs to renounce the specific words he or she said so that the covenant with the demonic is broken.

## FINDING EVERY KEY TO DELIVERANCE

It's important to talk with people to discover the doors they have opened, as the Holy Spirit leads you to minister to them and find every key needed to unlock their deliverance. In some cases, you might need an additional key, which the Holy Spirit will show you as you talk with the person. For example, some people might have been heavily involved in witchcraft or might have given a lot of money to the devil's kingdom (giving money to psychics, witch healers/doctors, etc.). In this case, they have sowed so much into the demonic kingdom that they have reaped mightily, and they are now in a deficit in the spiritual realm. Sowing into the Kingdom of God unlocks these specific chains; it removes this reaping and brings them out of the deficit. In other cases, an additional key to deliverance might be getting rid of any personal items that have to do with the occult, or being in the presence of a vessel with higher-level anointing to deliver.

Also, God may choose to deliver a person who has many demons in layers and in stages. For example, one day God may deliver a person from suicidal spirits, and later on He may then deliver that person from demons that came in when he or she was abused. We see in the Bible how a blind man gained some sight when Jesus spit on his eyes and placed His hands on him. And then Jesus prayed again and the man gained all of his sight (see Mark 8:22–26). Be patient with God's timing for delivering a person.

There also may be times when it appears that a person is still manifesting after you have commanded the demons to go. Yet actually, God is still in the process of delivering that person. It's not every time that all demons go immediately, at one time. The Holy Spirit will bring you discernment in such cases, and it's also important to be planted under a spiritual father/ mother who can give you further guidance about dealing with such cases, as needed.

I have also heard so many testimonies of people who were delivered in their dreams after a revival service. Others were delivered after they left a service. In the Bible, there's a story where ten men with leprosy were healed after they left Jesus (see Luke 17:11–19). The anointing of Jesus had come upon them and was working in them as they went on their way. Jesus is the same yesterday, today and forever. So in the same way as with the lepers, Jesus will sometimes deliver and heal people after the anointing is first released to them. When you are praying for people and it seems that demons are not going, it could be because of the above reason—that the anointing is working in them and they will be delivered over time. But other times, demons may not actually be leaving because a certain key in the spiritual realm first needs to be used to unlock a person's freedom. It could be that the person is not renouncing specifically enough. It could be that the person made a pact with the devil, or made a covenant of suicide that he or she must renounce specifically.

Also, the apostles Paul and Peter carried a high level of anointing that not everyone carried. This anointing dealt with higher-level demons like principalities. Another reason a demon might not go is because a higher level of anointing is required to cast out that higher-level demon. If a person's demonic bondage is deeper and the demons haven't left after you've prayed (based on following up with the person), it may be that there are such higher-level demons involved. In that case, help the person you're praying for find a church or ministry that has experience in deliverance and is anointed. He or she will find additional help there, where the anointing is flowing, just like in the Acts Church. It could even be online, if you don't know of a church in your location that operates in deliverance. Many people are learning, being discipled and receiving deliverance just as they're watching 5F Church's or other ministries' livestreams and replays.

So if you encounter a stubborn deliverance situation with people you're praying for, and you've been receiving an impartation of anointing from a certain place, it's important to share with such people that they should tune in to videos of that ministry to ensure that they receive help from vessels with high-level anointing to deal with the remaining high-level demons. Or if they're able, they should attend with you in person, and then they can also be discipled there. Also invite and encourage them to come to church regularly for equipping, impartation, more deliverance if needed and for fellowship with the Body of Christ.

When a person receives deliverance, it is important that he or she is equipped and discipled to know how to maintain that freedom and how to be strong in the spirit and victorious over the enemy. This discipling and equipping must come from true anointed ministries. If a person is delivered and then continues only to receive from a church that doesn't carry the anointing or provide "meaty" teachings to equip believers for victory over the devil, then the person will not be equipped to overcome the enemy's schemes of trying to come back with even more demons.

## HOW TO RELEASE ANOINTING TO HEAL

Behind many sicknesses is actually a demonic spirit. If the sickness/disease/disorder runs in your family, it is most likely a generational curse that needs to be broken.

Many times, a spirit of infirmity is behind a sickness. Jesus cast the deaf spirit out of a man, and the man could then hear. Jesus cast mute spirits out of people, and they could then speak. Some people with autism, or others who are nonverbal, may have a spirit of muteness that needs to be cast out.

When praying for someone with sickness, release the anointing to heal by doing these things:

1. Ask the person to renounce the sickness and any agreement with the sickness, as well as any generational curse.
2. Speak over the person, "I detach you from what you've renounced, and I command every spirit attached to you to come out." As God leads you, you can speak, "This sickness [i.e., name it as cancer, etc.] must leave this body completely." This is not a script to follow, but a general template. Follow the Holy Spirit in each case.
3. Speak out "I declare healing to you," or "Be healed." You can lay hands on the person, if God leads, or just declare healing over him or her, depending on how the Holy Spirit leads you. (This step isn't required every

time, as often the healing happens the moment the spirit is cast out. Other times God may lead you to declare healing without the renouncing and commanding a spirit of infirmity to leave.)

## HOW TO RELEASE ANOINTING AS YOU PREACH

The apostle Paul said this: "My message and my preaching were not with wise and persuasive words, but with a demonstration of the Spirit's power, so that your faith might not rest on human wisdom, but on God's power" (1 Corinthians 2:4–5). When I first received the prophecy that I was called to be an apostle, one of the greatest mysteries was how on earth I was going to preach and preach regularly. I loved listening to preachers, but I never, ever thought I would be able to preach myself. I didn't think that I could get profound revelation from God. I didn't even feel secure that I could hear Him all that well. I would look at other preachers and think, *Wow, how do they do that?*

So when I began preaching, my messages were simple— simply sharing what God had taught me, straightforward, without any bells and whistles. They were without extraordinary metaphors and elaborate illustrations. For about three years, Sunday after Sunday I would hear the devil's lies: *You aren't a good preacher. The people aren't being blessed.*

Recently, however, I have received many testimonies about how my simple preaching is helping people understand the Word of God for the first time. People have been saying that my simple preaching has led to so much spiritual growth for them because things aren't going over their heads and they can actually grasp what's being taught. Hearing this shocked me. I had this moment when I thought, *Wow, the devil is such a liar!* All this time, I thought my preaching wasn't good enough. But it turns out that it was exactly what some people needed, and exactly how God wanted to use me. It wasn't that God wasn't giving me enough "revelation." He was giving me exactly what He wanted these people to hear.

There is this pressure in the Christian world to be a charismatic, amazing preacher. But people don't need fancy preaching. They need the simple truth to set them free. They need anointed teaching that feeds their spirit, not their soul (their mind, will and emotions). Concerts, inspiring movies and inspirational speeches can feed your soul. They can uplift your mood and make you shed a tear. There is even preaching that just preaches to the soul, void of anointing. That kind of preaching doesn't bring lasting change to a person, however, only a temporary feeling. Anointed teaching feeds your spirit and makes your spirit grow and your carnal nature go down. Anointed teaching is what brings actual transformation.

Paul said he didn't come to people with wise, persuasive words, but with demonstrations of God's power. For many years, I listened to sermon after sermon filled with persuasive words about why I should believe in Jesus. None of those sermons actually led me to surrender to God. I raised my hand so many times, saying "I give everything to Jesus," but there was no change and I remained lukewarm. When I began to hear anointed teaching, however, my spirit leaped. My spirit had been fed, and it ignited such a fire in me. I surrendered everything to God. My faith was resting on God's power instead of on man's wisdom and persuasive words.

I am convinced that everyone can be a preacher. Everyone can preach the simple Gospel. Everyone can share what God has taught them, so other people can grow in faith. You don't need to be a charismatic, professional communicator to speak the Word of God. It's time we stop trying to look impressive and stop trying to get people riled up to say loud "Amens" that make us feel as if we are impressive preachers. It's time we have a heart for people to really encounter Jesus through us, and encounter His power. It's time we become passionate that people can be set free by the truth, the way we've been set free—by the simple truth, without unnecessary bells and whistles that only distract.

When you speak the Word of God, whether it's leading a Bible study, sharing the Word with just one person, or preaching up onstage in front of many, don't try to be like other preachers. The way God made you is unique, and it's just what the world needs. Be yourself. Speak normally. You don't have to preach loudly for the anointing to flow. The anointing flows most powerfully not when you're trying to perform and get a reaction, but when you're simply sharing the truth passionately from your heart, in the normal way in which you speak. You don't have to fake a "preacher" voice.

When you are authentically yourself, you spread revival the most powerfully, because people can see that they can just be themselves, too. Be honest about your weaknesses. Be vulnerable and share how you overcame attacks from the enemy. As you speak simply and honestly, the anointing will flow powerfully through you, and the power of God will touch people. God will use you to ignite hunger in them. God will use you to release faith to others so that they are ready to receive the miracle He wants to release to them.

Many times during a message I'm preaching, demons will start screaming out of people or manifesting in some way, and people will be delivered right there. It isn't a loud voice and hype coming out of me that makes the demons go, but rather the anointing flowing out of me while I am preaching the simple truth in a normal voice. The more we get out of the way and stop with the theatrics and hype, the more God can be seen. When we get in the way by giving a performance, we cover the glory of God.

When we make space for God to really be the center, however, His power will move so mightily. What we should desire is for people to leave a service filled with awe at God, and nothing else. They shouldn't leave thinking, *That was great music/lighting/performance/comedy/theatrical preaching.* . . . When you and I step back and allow God to be the center, all that people will be able to think about is, *Wow, Jesus, you are so amazing!*

# 11

# Maintaining the Anointing

The [reverent] fear of the LORD is the beginning (the
prerequisite, the absolute essential, the alphabet) of
wisdom;
A good understanding and a teachable heart are possessed
by all those who do the will of the LORD;
His praise endures forever.

Psalm 111:10 AMP

Throughout the Bible, we find examples of anointed servants of
God who maintained the anointing, and we also see examples
of those who lost the anointing. Once you have made it to the
"promised land" of walking in the anointing, there is no guar-
antee that you will be anointed forever. You have to continue
to be obedient to God in order for the anointing to stay and
for it to grow in you.

King Saul lost his anointing because he was disobedient
to God. He cared what people thought more than what God
thought. Judas was a close disciple of Jesus, but he stepped

away from his calling as an anointed vessel, betrayed Jesus with a kiss and then killed himself. Samson disobeyed God and gave away the secret between him and God, breaking the covenant of what made the anointing flow to him (see Judges 16:17). The anointing left him immediately.

We have to obey God, not people. Obeying Him brings favor and blessing in your life. Obedience is what brings the elevation. Don't focus on getting other people's attention and support, even if critics seem to come out of the woodwork. In all that criticism comes the temptation to obey people over God. But you don't need people to approve of you and open doors for you in order to fulfill your God-given purpose. God will open up every door, and no man or woman can shut those doors. Don't let your eyes wander on social media and obsess over what others are saying or doing. Stay focused on Jesus and all He is calling you to do.

## GOD BEFORE ALL ELSE

Your relationship with God must come first, before all else. Maintaining intimacy with God takes intention. Walking in the anointing is a life of revival, and revival gets busy! It's harvest time. God will fill so much of your time with His work, and it's such a good thing! So you have to be intentional about taking time just to be with God.

As you read the gospels, you find that Jesus was very hard at work, doing what the Father had assigned Him to do. But you also find Him regularly taking time to go away from the crowds, just to be alone with God.

Walking in the anointing comes with a busier schedule, especially when you're coming from a wilderness season. You must make it your serious intention to maintain intimacy with Jesus. Decide today that no matter what, you will always spend time with God daily. Decide now that you will make it your intention every day to focus your eyes on God throughout the activities of your daily life.

Make the decision never to drift away from the place of intimacy with God because your life gets too busy and too exciting.

*Nothing is more important than your relationship with Jesus.*

## KEEP YOUR HEART PURE

Keep your heart pure and free of offense. It's so important to keep your heart full of love for all people. When offense and bitterness creep in, it becomes an open door for the enemy. God made it clear that we *will* have haters and persecution. We are actually *blessed* when we are persecuted. The devil only goes after those who are anointed and dangerous to his kingdom.

Whenever I go through persecution, I remind myself, *I'm doing powerful things for the Kingdom, and God is proud of me. I'm making the devil mad. I'm going higher, and blessings are coming my way.* Persecution means eternal rewards here and in heaven.

As I said earlier, with new levels come new devils. The devil has all these different schemes and tricks for trying to stop anointed ones. You can't choose your battle, but you can choose how you respond to the battle. You will face different kinds of attacks on your journey of walking in the anointing. It's important to prepare for battle.

Even now, as you're reading this book, maybe you're just learning what the anointing is and you've just started on your journey to walk in it. Prepare for battle now. "Be alert and of sober mind. Your enemy the devil prowls around like a roaring lion looking for someone to devour" (1 Peter 5:8). Don't let the devil catch you off guard. Remind yourself that you are in a lifelong battle. You have the victory every time, but the way you are victorious is by being prepared and being aware of the devil's schemes.

Remind yourself of your purpose continually: to serve Jesus and please Him with everything you do. Everything must align with that purpose. You are not here to see your dreams come true. You are not here to be popular and likable. You are not here to fulfill your own desires. You are here to serve Jesus and touch His heart. If that means occasional persecution and trials, so be it. If that means mountaintops and valleys, so be it. Meditate on your purpose continually so it really goes deep in your heart. Whenever the devil attacks, you'll be prepared for victory, staying in God's will as you obey Him.

## SPIRITUAL PROTECTION UNDER YOUR COVERING

One of the most important keys to maintaining the anointing is to have a spiritual covering and "stay under" your covering. Your spiritual covering is your spiritual mother or father (your "Elijah," whom we talked about earlier). Your place of receiving the anointing is under your spiritual mother or father. Staying planted under that covering is what makes the anointing flow into your life, and it's also what makes the anointing continue to increase as you grow in it, going from glory to glory.

The apostle Paul speaks about spiritual fathers in 1 Corinthians 4:15 (NLT): "For even if you had ten thousand others to teach you about Christ, you have only one spiritual father. For I became your father in Christ Jesus when I preached the Good News to you." You can have several teachers who help you understand the Word of God, but you only have one spiritual father or mother.

Paul also talks about how he has a trustworthy son, Timothy: "For this reason I have sent to you Timothy, my son whom I love, who is faithful in the Lord. He will remind you of my way of life in Christ Jesus, which agrees with what I teach everywhere in every church" (1 Corinthians 4:17). Through this passage, you can see how Timothy was planted underneath the covering of his spiritual father, Paul, and was carrying the anointing as Paul's spiritual son.

You access spiritual protection when you stay under the covering. It's like when a child is inside his or her parents' house. No kidnapper can touch that child because the child is safe inside the locked house. That's the child's covering. When you don't have a covering, it's like when a child is outside the parents' house, on his or her own. A spiritual kidnapper could easily attack you when you're outside the covering God has provided for you. That high-level anointing flowing from your spiritual father or mother brings protection. In the spiritual realm, demons know they cannot touch you when you are obeying the spiritual laws of staying under your covering, where God has led you to stay planted.

Your anointing for ministry may be a lower-level anointing at first, but you are accessing the high-level anointing from your covering for spiritual protection. When you leave your covering, you are entering a dangerous place spiritually, and you are proving untrustworthy. There can, however, be times when you are under one covering and then God leads you to move under a different covering. We are all on a journey, and anointing is rare. You may be on a journey right now of seeking God and asking Him who your spiritual father and/or mother should be. Seek the Lord, and He will be faithful to answer and lead you perfectly.

Once God has made where you should be planted clear to you, stay safely planted under that covering. Then, acknowledge your covering and help people understand the importance of having a covering themselves. When people fully know the principles of how to receive the anointing, and how important it is to stay under a spiritual covering, more and more pure vessels will carry and grow in the anointing.

## GIVE HONOR WHERE HONOR IS DUE

Give respect to whom respect is due, and honor to whom honor is due (see Romans 13:7). As God lifts you, never forget where you came from. God is using you powerfully now because there was someone who went before you and poured into you, discipling you, mentoring you and imparting the anointing in you.

I look back on the transformation that occurred in my life, and I am amazed. I have grown so tremendously from where I first began. It was God who transformed me, but He chose to use a vessel to teach me and impart the anointing to me. My spiritual father taught me so much, and because he was obedient to God, I was able to receive from God through him. He sacrificed and poured so much into me for the sake of the Kingdom. He has such a heart for the whole Body of Christ to be operating in the anointing. He is the most selfless person I have ever met.

I always remind myself that I'm not walking in the anointing now because I'm "so great" or because of my obedience alone. It's because there was an "Elijah" who went before me, who went through so much himself that now I can stand strong as I look at his example. I can look at how he went through persecution and follow his example so I can make it through. God proved He was with my spiritual father, so God will prove He is with me, too. Seeing my spiritual father's Christlike example has helped mold my heart to be more Christlike. As Paul says, "Follow my example, as I follow the example of Christ" (1 Corinthians 11:1). God used my spiritual father to help me know how to walk in authority and cast out demons. I'm eternally grateful for his obedience to God, and for his love for God and His Kingdom. That obedience and love have enabled my spiritual father to pour out so much to me and to the Body of Christ.

I also recognize other vessels of God in my life who helped me get to where I am today. Jeanntal has stood by my side since the first year I began 5F Church. Just as David had Jonathan as a loyal best friend and supporter in God's work, God gave me Jeanntal. I went through many difficult trials when it would have been easy to give up, but she was always there, supporting me as a reminder of God's faithfulness. For years, she was usually the only one who was telling me that my preaching touched her week after week. I don't know what I would have done without her encouragement.

I honor my parents, too, who have supported me my whole entire life, in every way! When I told them God was calling me to be an apostle and start a church, they supported me. There were years when week after week I didn't know how we would pay for the church rent, and year after year my parents supported the ministry financially. Even though this way of doing ministry was different than what they had known from their Presbyterian/Baptist background, they never came to me with doubt or skepticism. They always trusted God's hand over my life. God used them as pillars of support in every area from emotional to financial, and I can't imagine how I would have made it without their support.

## STAY HUMBLE AND GRATEFUL

Always give glory to God as He lifts you. Remind yourself continually that the anointing you carry and the blessings you have received are only by the grace of God. You are not entitled to them because of "what you sacrificed" and "how hard you worked" for God. When people in the world have success, money and fame, many times they feel entitled to it because of how hard they worked. They think, *Of course I have this. I worked so hard for it!* But we as believers must be different when the blessings flow. Every blessing is a pure gift from God. We don't deserve even to have breath; it was God's grace that He brought us to life and gave us breath, along with every other blessing in this life.

God is lifting you for His glory. He blesses you because He loves you, yes. But the bigger reason He blesses you and lifts you is so your light may become brighter, so more people can be attracted to your light, where they will find Him. "You are the light of the world. A city that is set on a hill cannot be hidden" (Matthew 5:14 NKJV). As God lifts you, stay humble and grateful, and remind yourself that every single blessing is for a purpose—God's glory. Don't treat your blessings as yours alone, but as blessings that God is entrusting you to steward well and use for a purpose.

When God lifts you, there are great blessings in store. But with new elevation come new challenges and different obstacles to overcome. In a new season of elevation will come a challenge you didn't have in the previous season. For me, I found more resistance from the devil than ever. I could see that the enemy was angry. I have had to choose not to give the devil and his distractions any attention. He will try to distract you from the blessings God has given you and the mission God has assigned you to carry out. Don't give the devil the time of day, and don't let him steal your joy!

Remember to keep your focus on Jesus and continually thank God for all He has blessed you with and for His faithfulness. In the midst of trials, thank God in advance for His victory over the situation. Stay humble as God lifts you and promises come to pass. Make it your practice to remember where He brought you from. When you are feeling anxious for the next promise to come to pass, remember how you used to long for the promise that you are living in now!

## REMAIN TEACHABLE

Another important key to maintaining the anointing is always to stay teachable. When God first uses you in the anointing, you are far from knowing everything about the spiritual realm.

Many times, God will start to use you for a specific purpose and will give you much spiritual knowledge and wisdom on that particular thing. And then a new season may come when God wants to use you in a new way, and when there is much you have to learn. He takes you step by step so you always need to rely on Him. He purposefully doesn't share everything with you at one time, so you can keep your childlike dependence on Him. Just because you've known the Lord for a long time doesn't mean you have all the spiritual insight in the world. God is using the foolish things to confound the wisdom of this world right now, in this revival (see again 1 Corinthians 1:27).

God chooses to reveal Kingdom things to those who are childlike: "At that time Jesus prayed this prayer: "O Father, Lord of heaven and earth, thank you for hiding these things from those who think themselves wise and clever, and for revealing them to the childlike" (Matthew 11:25 NLT). There is so much God has yet to reveal to us as we age spiritually. The moment you lose your childlike, teachable spirit, you shut yourself off from receiving spiritual revelation from Him. You really must stay in that same childlike, teachable place that you began with, when God first saw that He could trust you with the anointing. You need to stay there your whole life and actually become more and more humble and teachable.

God will surprise you in the ways He teaches you. He may teach you through a person much younger than you in physical age, or through someone who has been a Christian for a lot less time than you. Remain teachable enough that God can teach you something through such a person.

When God starts to use someone else in a new way, be teachable, not prideful. You should think, *Wow, that person must be childlike for God to reveal new revelation, and for him (or her) to be walking in the power of God like that.* I humble myself: *Lord, teach me. I have so much to learn. Teach me in whatever way you want. I want to be used mightily by you. I know there is so much more.*

## TAKE CARE OF YOURSELF

"Do you not know that your bodies are temples of the Holy Spirit, who is in you, whom you have received from God? You are not your own; you were bought at a price. Therefore honor God with your bodies" (1 Corinthians 6:19–20). Your body is a temple that the anointing resides in. You only get one temple. You must take care of this temple. When God lifts you, you have to take extra care to make sure your temple is healthy and protected.

Your spirit, soul and body are all connected. As God lifts you, be aware that the devil wants to find a loophole where he can attack you and drain the anointing. You need to take care of your spirit, soul and body to make sure that the anointing itself is protected. Let's look at each of these areas more closely.

### Taking Care of Your Spirit

To maintain the anointing, it's important to live a pure and holy life. Live a life obeying God, staying in His Word, staying in relationship with Him and doing work for His Kingdom. Stay focused on these things and give your all. Don't get distracted with the things of the world. Your every decision should come from the place of *Is this pleasing to God?*

When you are walking in the anointing, the fear of God should arise in you. He has entrusted you with so much. Protect the anointing and your spiritual health with your life. End the relationships God is asking you to end. Cherish every day as a holy day, a day for you to please and serve the Lord. Don't waste time; rather, spend each moment with purpose. Humble yourself regularly and make it your practice to thank God and spend time worshiping Him.

You shouldn't let just anyone lay hands on you. It's big in Western Church culture for everyone to lay hands on one another. But I have seen many people who needed deliverance from spirits such as witchcraft or demonic tongues because someone else claiming to be a Christian laid hands on them, and/or they fully accepted a prophecy from such a person in their hearts. If you don't know someone, you don't need to allow that person to place their hand on you if they ask. If someone prays for you and God is convicting you in your heart that you shouldn't accept the prayer, don't accept it.

Walk in wisdom about accepting prayers and prophecies. It's not spiritually wise to accept prophecies just everywhere. Not everyone who claims to prophesy does so with God's wisdom. When someone wants to prophesy for the wrong reasons (for example, to look spiritually important), that opens a door for a psychic spirit. When you accept prophecies from just anywhere, it can be dangerous for your spiritual health and for the anointing you're carrying. It can be a way that the enemy will come in with confusion and redirect you out of God's will.

Part of being a trustworthy vessel is that you are someone who walks with wisdom and honors his or her covering. Walking in wisdom means not receiving prophecy just because you want to hear more and more prophecy. Walking in wisdom means that you don't treat receiving prophecy and prayer like eating at a buffet. It is wisdom to go only where God has led you to receive prophecy, prayer and direction.

### Taking Care of Your Soul

"Do not conform to the pattern of this world, but be transformed by the renewing of your mind. Then you will be able to test and approve what God's will is—his good, pleasing and perfect will" (Romans 12:2). You need to renew your soul continually by reminding yourself of God's truth. Your soul is where the devil's lies sneak in. You need to be on guard for these lies and keep your soul protected and flourishing.

A big area where I noticed the devil used to attack me in my soul was in my confidence in my relationship with God. Before I encountered God's power and had a revelation of His love, I would hear this voice in my mind telling me all the time: *You're not being a good enough Christian. You're not reading your Bible enough. You're not praying enough. God is disappointed.* Walking in relationship with God and being confident in His love for you are foundational to being a powerful vessel of God. So the devil comes in a sneaky way to try to tear down your confidence, making you feel unworthy of carrying the anointing and afraid that you'll lose the anointing. It's important that you are aware of this scheme so you don't fall for the devil's lies.

The spirit of religion screams, *You need to pray _____ hours (this amount of time)! You need to read _____ chapters (this amount) of the Bible! You need to do _____ (this and this and this) to be a good Christian!* No one can measure up to what the spirit of religion demands. But being in good relationship with God simply means obeying Him, serving Him, communing with Him throughout your days and spending time in the Word and in prayer with Him as He leads. It isn't about a certain amount of prayer or Bible reading.

God's love language is obedience. Whenever you are obeying God, you are touching His heart the very most. When you are doing something as simple as cleaning your house, if that's what God has asked you to do in that moment, you are touching His heart the very most. Sometimes we get stuck in the religious mindset of *I'm only pleasing God when I'm reading the Bible and praying.* But that's not true. God is with you all day, every day. He is loving on you every step of the way, and you are touching His heart and being intimate with Him even when you are doing the mundane things of life, when that's what He is asking you to do.

So much of my life is spent in service to God, doing active work for His Kingdom. There are some days when what God has called me to do means there is less time to spend in quietness with Him (for example, on a full day of travel). I have to remind myself that what touches His heart is my obedience. Period. I have to remind myself not to be religious. I have to remind myself that God loves me so much and that He is proud of me. To keep your soul healthy, you have to remind yourself of these truths.

The more spiritually minded you can be, the more powerfully the anointing will flow from you. When I realized this, I knew my mindset had to shift completely. Instead of thinking, *I need to protect the health of my soul for myself,* I shifted to the greater purpose of staying healthy to minister. This became a great responsibility, and my mindset shifted to thinking, *I need to protect the health of my soul so I can serve God and minister to others.*

Another way the devil tries to attack the anointing is by stealing your peace. There will be many temptations to become stressed, but being stressed is a choice. You can actually choose to have perfect peace. Perfect peace is part of the inheritance Jesus has given you: "You will keep him in perfect peace, whose mind is stayed on you, because he trusts in You" (Isaiah 26:3 NKJV).

When stressful situations arise, renew your mind immediately with the Word of God: "For God has not given us a spirit of fear and timidity, but of power, love, and self-discipline" (2 Timothy 1:7 NLT).

Remind yourself that there is nothing to fear. God is in control. He is protecting you and has made prosperous plans for you: "'For I know the plans I have for you,' declares the LORD, 'plans to prosper you and not to harm you, plans to give you hope and a future'" (Jeremiah 29:11).

Nothing can stop God's plans for your life. The promises *will* come to pass. God will scatter your enemies: "The LORD will conquer your enemies when they attack you. They will attack you from one direction, but they will scatter from you in seven!" (Deuteronomy 28:7 NLT).

This trial and this pain are only temporary: "Weeping may endure for a night, but joy comes in the morning" (Psalm 30:5 NKJV). As it was with Job, God will restore all that the devil has stolen from you, and so much more.

Many times when I feel the devil's lies about stress coming on, when things are uncertain and out of my control, I remind myself that God absolutely is using this "threat of stress" moment to refine me some more. It's another test I have to pass that will lead to elevation for His glory. God needs us to be absolutely full of His presence, full of peace. The way God refines us to be full of perfect peace is to take us through the fiery furnace of trials tempting us toward stress. When I remind myself that God is refining me, it keeps me in perfect peace and I rest in His faithfulness.

### Taking Care of Your Body

Your soul is connected to your body. When you allow stress to take hold of your soul, your body will follow. Physical panic attacks, fainting, migraines, etc., can come when you are under stress. There was one time when I was going through the fiercest spiritual attack I've ever been through. I kept my peace and trusted God all through it, but my body and soul had been undergoing something traumatic—more traumatic than I had ever experienced before. One day during this attack, I could feel physically in my body the effects of the stress I had been under. I had never felt the physical effects of stress in my life. I thought I had done well keeping my peace and not letting the trauma of the attacks get to me, but this experience taught me that going forward, I need to take *extra* care of my soul. Otherwise, my body will be negatively affected. For example, I need to make sure never to meditate on bad words being spoken about me. I need to be careful about what I am intaking on social media and make sure only to dwell on the good:

> Finally, brothers and sisters, whatever is true, whatever is noble, whatever is right, whatever is pure, whatever is lovely, whatever is admirable—if anything is excellent or praiseworthy—think about such things.
>
> Philippians 4:8

The devil will try to bring stress in different ways. Make sure you are aware of your thoughts. If you are sensing many negative, fearful or stressful thoughts, make a decision to put a stop to this attack of the devil: "Submit yourselves therefore to God. Resist the devil, and he will flee from you" (James 4:7 ESV). Resist the devil's lies and take captive every fearful, depressed, stressful, negative thought. Again, this is not only for mental peace, but because what's going on in your soul so greatly affects what's going on in your body.

You have to be like a police officer on duty, constantly policing your thoughts, or just like with disturbances in society, there can be collateral damage. "We demolish arguments and every pretension that sets itself up against the knowledge of God, and we take captive every thought to make it obedient to Christ" (2 Corinthians 10:5). Don't allow negative thoughts to run rampant and bring destruction in your mind and body. Take them captive and make them obedient to Christ! You can speak things like these out loud:

"All negative, anxious thoughts must get out of my mind!"
"I have a sound mind."
"Jesus has given me perfect peace."

"Thank you, Jesus, for being in control of my life. You are working all things out for the good!"

"Lord, you are on my side, so who can be against me?"

"I can do all things through Christ who strengthens me!"

Remove from your life whatever causes negativity to build. Cut down on or fast from social media, and unfollow accounts that lead to stress. Make sure you aren't complaining and speaking negatively, which open the door for the devil to bring even more negative thoughts to your mind. Make it your intention to focus on the good. Meditate on God's faithfulness, His blessings on your life, His Word and His promises.

It is also important to take care of your physical health in practical ways. Sleep is very important for the health of your body and soul. Sleep is important to being full of peace, joy and the fire of God. When my schedule began to get busier than ever, I had to be intentional like never before to plan my days so that I was getting enough sleep. There will be a day or week when you just can't get a lot of sleep because of the schedule God has you on, and He will give you supernatural energy. But this shouldn't be something you take advantage of and depend on. When God's schedule for you allows, make sure you're getting the proper rest so He can use you without anything holding you back.

It is important to exercise when you can. Make it a habit to spend at least half an hour most days doing something active. I love to be out in nature, so I go for a walk or a run outside most days.

It is also important to eat well and drink ample amounts of water. Eat food that won't weigh you down, but will help nourish your body.

God has plans to give you a long life and use you mightily all the days of your life. You need to take care of your body to preserve it for the Lord's use. You are so valuable to Him. Value your temple, your body! Taking care of your body is being obedient to God and is touching His heart as well.

## WALK IN THE ANOINTING OF GOD

As I conclude this book, I feel as though I have poured out all my secrets, everything I have learned so far about how to carry anointing. My heart and assignment from God are to share what He has taught me with you, so that you can also walk in the power of God.

*Revival Is Now* and God is ready to use you wherever you are! If you apply what you have learned in these pages, there is no doubt that God will use you mightily in His anointing. The heart of God is for you to freely give, as you have freely received (see again Matthew 10:8). These secrets I have shared carry keys that unlock revival that can spread across the whole world— revival where it's not just one person carrying the anointing, but all believers who have pure, trustworthy hearts.

I encourage you to keep this book available so you can return to it when needed. You might be at step one of walking in the anointing now, but as you reach different stages along the journey, return to whatever chapter God is taking you through. For example, in the wilderness season, return to the wilderness chapter to empower you. On occasion, return to this chapter about maintaining the anointing, so no scheme of the enemy can take away the precious anointing growing inside you.

Now it is time to begin your journey—or to continue your journey—of walking in the anointing. You are a world changer. You are a warrior in God's end-time revival army. Heaven is cheering you on! God is so proud of you!

You are a chosen one. Many are called, and few are chosen. You are chosen! Get ready for the very best days of your life.

Get ready for a life of awe and wonder. Get ready to live a supernatural life, full of miracles every single day!

I declare this anointing to come upon you now: Be filled with the power of God that destroys every kind of yoke. I declare that as you pray for the sick, they will be healed. I declare that demons will tremble in your presence and will obey your command and leave people who are oppressed. I declare that spiritually blind eyes will be opened through you. I declare that the lukewarm will be set on fire through you. As people come into your presence, may they encounter God's power and have a revelation of His love for them. I declare that you are a revival carrier. May revival spread through you like a wildfire! Nothing can stop God's plan to use you in His anointing. *Revival is in you now!* Go out and spread the revival fire to the world!

**Kathryn Krick** is the lead pastor of Five-Fold Church (5F Church) in Los Angeles, California, where many miracles happen and people are healed, delivered, receive impartation and are transformed by God's power. Several travel from all over the world to encounter God at 5F Church weekly.

Kathryn has large and rapidly growing YouTube, Facebook, Instagram and Tiktok audiences where several thousand receive miracles as they watch her live services and videos online. She also travels around the world ministering at Revival events where thousands encounter God. Her greatest passion is to see others encounter God's power and have revelation of His love.

Kathryn makes her home in Los Angeles. Find out more about her, and about 5F Church, at:

www.5fchurch.org
www.apostlekathrynkrick.com
www.youtube.com/ApostleKathrynKrick
www.facebook.com/apostlekathrynkrick
www.instagram.com/apostlekathrynkrick/